D1588391

John Grant was the co-founder of London creative agency St Luke's, as famous for its free-range office, ethics and employee co-ownership as for its creative work for clients like Body Shop, IKEA and the BBC. He has published six previous business books on brands, sustainability, innovation and globalization, all written to celebrate fresh ideas, bold experiments, spirit and change. He has advised ethical companies such as Innocent, Method/Ecover, Eden and Ecotricity on how to grow bigger; and others, such as IKEA, Samsung, Unilever and Pepsi on how to be more human, relevant and lovable. He lives in Highgate, London.

By the same author

New Marketing Manifesto 1999

After Image 2002

Brand Innovation Manifesto 2005

Green Marketing Manifesto 2007

Co-opportunity 2010

Made With 2014

wellbeeing and
human-friendly business

BETTƎR

by john grant

Unbound

This edition first published in 2018

Unbound
6th Floor Mutual House, 70 Conduit Street, London W1S 2GF

www.unbound.com

Text Design by Ellipsis

A CIP record for this book is available from the British Library

ISBN 978-1-78352-568-3 (trade hbk)

ISBN 978-1-78352-569-0 (ebook)

ISBN 978-1-78352-567-6 (limited edition)

Printed in Great Britain by CPI Group (UK)

Heartfelt thanks to the swarm of bees that made this book possible. To Faizia and Shumi for the visual loveliness. To Anna, Georgia, Jimmy, John, Kwaku and Lauren for their Unbounded enthusiasm. To Jane, Will and others who discussed the early concept and helped me give it a direction. And to all the generous supporters, listed later in this book.

Dear Reader,

The book you are holding came about in a rather different way to most others. It was funded directly by readers through a new website: Unbound. Unbound is the creation of three writers. We started the company because we believed there had to be a better deal for both writers and readers. On the Unbound website, authors share the ideas for the books they want to write directly with readers. If enough of you support the book by pledging for it in advance, we produce a beautifully bound special subscribers' edition and distribute a regular edition and ebook wherever books are sold, in shops and online.

This new way of publishing is actually a very old idea (Samuel Johnson funded his dictionary this way). We're just using the internet to build each writer a network of patrons. At the back of this book, you'll find the names of all the people who made it happen.

Publishing in this way means readers are no longer just passive consumers of the books they buy, and authors are free to write the books they really want. They get a much fairer return too – half the profits their books generate, rather than a tiny percentage of the cover price.

If you're not yet a subscriber, we hope that you'll want to join our publishing revolution and have your name listed in one of our books in the future. To get you started, here is a £5 discount on your first pledge. Just visit unbound.com, make your pledge and type wellbeeing5 in the promo code box when you check out.

Thank you for your support,

Dan, Justin and John

Founders, Unbound

let's start with a simple question.
What are organisations for?

Finding the purpose of your business is in fashion.
Just look at corporates like Unilever with its Sustainable
Living Plan. Or M&S with its Plan A. Or at challengers
born clutching a vision. Like Tesla's aim to 'accelerate
the transition to renewable energy'. Those examples
relate to sustainability. But others have found their
reason to be in welfare – using the business to help
develop societies and not just their own self-interest.
Like Microsoft 4Africa, or Vodafone and empowering
women. Some simply state their broad purpose
as 'improving life'; like IKEA, or Dow Chemicals.

Having an overt ambition that people can identify
with is a powerful thing. It's inspiring. Internally it can
stir people to bigger efforts. And make these feel part
of a bigger picture. Externally it signals you aren't
just motivated by self-interest. And that's important in
building trust. But in less progressive companies these
Purpose exercises however well meaning can be hollow.
They are stuck on, like a tail pinned on the donkey in the
children's game. Are imposed or post-rationalised
whereas proper company purpose is bred in the bone.

For most businesses – just as for an individual –
a rational ambition is not enough. It can only lead
to deep progress if it goes beyond head and into
heart. Without heart, after all, ambition can actually
be cruel. Purpose is an intellectual exercise unless
people feel it at an emotional level, are drawn in
by it. The company structures we have inherited are
technocratic, rational, machine-like and the whole
point of finding a human purpose is to turn it back
into an exciting collective quest.

Back at the question. What are organisations for?
The answer is: to care.

People join or deal with an organisation, or in fact
any social group, because they hope to be better
looked after (cherished, provided for, served, supported,
protected...) and to fare better than they would on their
own. I'm not just talking about having a predictable
salary and health benefit schemes. I mean quality
of life benefits too. Living fully. Flourishing. Achieving.
Connecting. Thriving. Enjoying your work and life
to the full and being shielded from peril.

care is why individuals give up individual
interests and freedoms and throw in their lot with
a group. It's an evolutionary thing. Survival of the
friendliest. It starts from the moment we are born
helpless and dependent. We live our lives in a delicate
web of human consideration, sympathy and kindnesses.
We aren't the only social species. Ants, bees and
beavers all do it. At some point in the past they may
have banded together for safety in numbers. The most
basic part of being cared for when we are infants is to
stay alive. But then opportunities emerged from living
in groups. Ants break up the earth and farm with aphids
and fungi instead of tractors. Beavers build their dams
and harvest a whole ecosystem of their own making.
Those group activities add hugely to the life chances
of individuals and also to their whole ecosystem.
The better the flowers do, the better the bees do too.

So before any business plan or purpose statement is
ever written... the organisation already has a purpose:
to care for its members and its communities. If not
why bother to associate with it, or buy from it, let alone

work for it? Many more people are choosing life in the freelance 'gig economy' as they aren't convinced corporate life will deliver on this implicit promise.

Some organisations have always known that care is the heart of a great business. IKEA for example defines its vision as: improve the everyday life of the majority of people. But most organisations don't seem to realise this. They see their enterprise as a kind of financial engine whirring to produce results. Or they grasp the importance of care only in fragments like HR policies and sustainability programmes.

Care may not be recognised as the purpose of every enterprise. But it is a powerful unwritten law: care for people or face their desertion. Just think what companies that endanger or damage our welfare do with a food poisoning, fraud or safety scare. They let their side of this deal down in such a fundamental way, that many never recover. You even see collapses when companies let just one customer's wellbeing down. For instance when United Airlines broke Dave Carroll's guitar. Worse than the event – accidents happen – was their uncaring response to his complaint. Dave's YouTube video mobilised millions of supporters, became a media relations crisis and knocked 9% off their share price.

Care is also how people instinctively value companies. Not by their share price. But by their overall contribution to human welfare, progress and quality of life. A soft drinks company may be one of the most profitable corporations on earth. But if they lose their legitimacy over care for our health, as many feel they are doing right at this moment, then they face challenging times ahead.

every food and drink company is having to rapidly recalibrate to a public which demands more care about what we eat. That what we eat is natural, without junk ingredients that do us harm. And also that it is lovingly crafted and served by people who care about its quality. It's not like every meal is a salad. But the world has turned to more authentic companies that care, even for fast food, or a quick hit of coffee. The world is walking out of Burger King and into Nando's, Leon, Chipotle. It's no longer enough to just factory produce something superficially filling, cheap and tasty.

There is plenty of room for companies to build a better quality of life through their core products and services. McDonalds in the UK is actually a shining example of striving to be better – from salads to sustainable sourcing to funky restyled cafes. And it has thrived commercially as a result. In marked contrast with McDonalds in the USA which did not change and is being deserted by millennials en masse. People still aspire and want to enjoy a better quality of life, but 'shiny' isn't enough. Today we have doubts about even the shiniest consumer baubles. Are our smart phones too addictive and too demanding, for instance? So saying 'we make X and people really love X' is not enough. What is your net contribution to life? Is 'X' really a big step for mankind?

The postwar boom that brought consumer goods into a world of scarcity was genuinely serving people's quality of life needs. But in a world where we have reached 'Peak Stuff' (as Steve Howard at IKEA puts it) what then? How then do you demonstrate the value of care? You have to make a leap. Organisations like Samsung, Deloitte have chosen to link their performance to the UN Sustainable Development Goals. Putting care at the heart of their accounting.

to summarise companies

that care deeply about people, that are human friendly rather than purely financial are increasingly recognised as having our interests at heart rather than just their own. And for reasons explored later in this book like Transparency, Talent and a growing deficit in Trust, this difference in culture is starting to make all the difference to reputation, recruitment, relationships with regulators and so on.

So if you are to care, what should you concern yourself with? Part of the answer is be relevant to what you do.

If you make household cleaners you might care for clean air, allergies, hygiene. If you make books or newspapers you might want to help people to read more. Whereas if you make sportswear you might care for our motivation and exercise. But there are some broader general headings that come from the basic dimensions of need – what humans everywhere generally need to have in their lives to flourish. I call these 5 core concerns H.E.A.R.T. which stands (as an acronym) for the drivers of human wellbeing. Not just Health (that's the h). But a range of factors we need for wellbeing drawn from researchers and social scientists.

This multifaceted definition of wellbeing goes back to the World Health Organisation definition of health as "a state of complete physical, mental, and social wellbeing and not merely the absence of disease or infirmity." Research later in the book shows that not having enough social connections later in life increases mortality rates by as much as smoking. Similarly the classic life stress scale by Holmes and Rahe shows that major life change events (positive and negative) like marriage, retirement and prison correlate with vulnerability to physical illnesses over the following few years. So while other wellbeing factors cover much more than health, they do impact on our health. A lot of attention recently has focused on stress, anxiety, vitality and emotional or mental health. Poor wellbeing in these areas erodes quality of life and restricts life chances.

how to define wellbeing – which is the nexus and result of all of these needs being met?

The New Economics Foundation defines wellbeing in broad terms as 'doing well, feeling good'.

The Centre of Development Studies at Bath offered a more comprehensive checklist of factors, including: standard of living, income, wealth and assets, employment and livelihood activities, education and skills, physical health and (dis)ability, environment quality, relations of love and care, networks of support and obligation, social, political and cultural identities and inequalities, violence, conflict and (in)security, a personal sense of agency, religious and moral frameworks, self-concept and personality, aspirations, a sense of meaning, satisfaction, trust and confidence.

The sense is that no matter how long this list, there would be more to add to it. Later in the book, for instance, we explore studies showing that access to nature has a strong effect on mood, lowers aggression and even increases memory and attention. National cultures can carry a culture of wellbeing – for instance Danish Hygge or Costa Rican Pura Vida. How happy (or indeed how fat) our immediate personal contacts are seems to be 'contagious'.

I have adapted my five headings from a sensible 5-item list used by Gallup Healthways, whose comprehensive survey of global wellbeing features later in this book:

H is for health.

E is for economics.

A is for ambition (or purpose).

R is for relationships.

T is for tribe (or community).

Each of these drivers has a huge impact on quality of life, on happiness, on human flourishing. Companies can have a big impact on each, especially businesses that embody the value of care.

Physical health. Problems of obesity, anxiety and other modern challenges are why the USA only ranks 23rd in Gallup Healthways ranking on national wellbeing, despite having such a lead on economic wellbeing. Little wonder nearly 80% of American organisations are investing in programs supporting worker health.

Economic wellbeing. This isn't necessarily just a case of more salary equals more happiness. In fact the average USA millennial says they would trade $7600 for a better quality of life at work. What people want is financial freedom. A sense of control of their destiny.

It's why consumers across the world are moving from being weighed down by owning loads of stuff to renting, sharing and favouring experiences.

Ambition. I talked already about companies having a purpose. And this is vital for individual wellbeing too. A large scale study in the USA and Japan found that those with a strong sense of purpose had a mortality rate one fifth lower. One fifth! Imagine a vitamin was discovered that reduced your chances of dying by one fifth, this year and every future year?

Relationships. There is growing recognition that wellbeing comes mostly from social factors. Whereas our medical and welfare models have tended to look at individual factors like 'lifestyle'. A lack of social connections correlates strongly with conditions like depression. According to a report in the Harvard Medical Review it is as risky in old age to lack strong relationships as it is to smoke 15 cigarettes a day.

Tribe. We are a social species and feel lost without tribes. Not just 'community' as in neighbourhoods. But groups with strong affinity, affiliation, living in each others' affairs; whether that's a little league team or a silicon valley start-up. Somewhere you feel you belong.

all these factors are interdependent.

It's hard to experience meaningfulness without a rich web of social relationships and community affiliations. It's also hard to do so when physical health is poor or money worries pressing. Conversely finding a new sense of purpose and self worth can lead you into new relationships and communities, help overcome health difficulties, and so on. The Bath Centre report points

out that wellbeing is a useful concept because
it is holistic; overcoming divisions in 'the modernist
understandings of the person' and promising
to connect mind, body and spirit.

The checklist isn't only of interest to policymakers
and academics. Whenever you look closer at great
companies that are trailblazing, spirited and great
places to work, you will often find a rich mix of all
five types of wellbeing being contributed to.
They are positively brimming with HEART.

about this book let's meet
a few few examples that feature later in the book:

LEON is the authentic, foodie, funky cafe chain that set
out to reinvent fast food. 'Why can't fast food be good
food?' asked the founders. And it is. Yummy. Playful.
Nutritious. Like their fish finger wrap. Behind the scenes
they are working on getting us into more plant-based
choices. Creating options for new diets like Paleo and
free-from. Taking nitrates out of chorizo. Care isn't just
about welfarism: it's also pride in what you make, how
you do things. Everything about LEON has HEART
because they care so much about every detail.

Natura Cosmetics, Brazil. Natura's slogan is 'bem estar
bem' – wellbeing well. It doesn't translate too well into
English; in Portuguese it means wellbeing and doing
good in a connected, holistic way. Not only do Natura
make fabulous soaps and cosmetics and perfumes.
Nor are they just known for being one of the most
innovative and most sustainable companies on earth.
But they also employ a giant tribe of 3 million

consultants, like the Avon ladies, who they see (like the historical co-operative movement, taking an interest in people's personal and economic development) as 'a movement'. When working with the company I visited a meeting of these consultants in a favela in Rio. And the beautiful thing (as one of the founders told me when we spoke about it) is that it's not charity; it's women developing themselves and supporting their families by selling stuff that they love.

Outdoor Voices is billed as "the next Nike". But their values couldn't be more different. Where Nike shouts "Just Do It" like an aggressive trackside coach, Outdoor Voices suggests we #dosomething. As their female millennial founder Tyler Haney explains: "It's a non-prescriptive call to action. Every other activewear brand champions this competitive, performance-driven ethos of faster, better, stronger. We believe that Doing Things is better than not doing things. The goal is to integrate activity into your life in a way that's approachable, social and fun." Companies with HEART tend to make great brands because they are exuberantly, authentically themselves. Outdoor Voices was named after being told to "shhh!" by parents when growing up, who would say "use your indoor voice."

Companies with HEART also bake wellbeing into their vision, mission, citizenship. Yes Outdoor Voices is into fitness, but so is Nike. The difference is HEART. Later in the book we will see trailblazing examples like Method who in addition to clearing our homes of chemical nasties and lightening our environmental footprints have also built a model factory to help regenerate Chicago's Pullman district. And in all of these cases they also put their care into delightful products, thoughtful innovations, gorgeous design and so on.

and finally one more question...

why now? Why is it suddenly so natural to be talking about human friendly business when ten years ago that was a fringe, and in the mainstream 'business is business'? Why is there the 'inexorable rise' of this book's subtitle? No longer is human friendly business a fringe. It's now centre stage. And these trends – like mindfulness, rebuilding trust and the ethic of care – have reached the heart of the establishment, for instance at the superpower grade business summits at Davos.

There could be all sorts of reasons for the shift. Health challenges like obesity and anxiety reaching a tipping point of concern? Millennials demanding work life balance and willing to change jobs to get it? The pace of life and work in an always-on society? Positive trends in lifestyles like yoga, clean eating seeping into the workplace? Business pressure like trust, transformation, transparency. The advancement of women and decline of traditional hierarchy.

And you know what? It's probably all of the above. Things on this scale tend to change in systems, rather than from one cause. But clearly as we will see in page after page and example after example this is fundamentally a shift in business culture. Not just in what business does but how it sees itself, and the way it goes about things. One way to think about cultures (from anthropologist Margaret Mead) is they always have a tree trunk concept. One core value against which others are measured. A value whose worth and explanatory power gets pride of place.

It is not hard to argue that the old tree trunk of business culture was competition. Since Adam Smith it was seen the "hidden hand" of economies. Being "competitive" has become synonymous with being a healthy business. I will argue what is happening today in business is a shift from competition to the tree trunk concept of care. This shift goes well beyond business. In consumer culture for instance, care is eclipsing cool. Where cool sought to be better than others (the consumer culture version of competition), care is about being better with others. According to philosopher Leonardo Buff "care is the central category of the new paradigm of civilization that is emerging worldwide". It is to be seen in sustainability, in the sharing economy, in social media, in the liberal values of milllennials worldwide, in social change movements. It can be discerned in a softening of fashion, architecture, food culture, localism, experiences.

That's the core message of this book. A shift from business as mechanical pursuit of competitive results, to business as a spirited human quest grounded in care for people. We have a long way to go. But any change for the better is an improvement and paves the way for much bigger changes to come.

built to blast

what the trump?

who moved my mouse

bodge

the war on talent

a new kind of business book
for a new era of business

We've reached the end of the production line. And we are into a new phase. When business is becoming human friendly again.

Before the industrial revolution, business used to be part of life. Baking was done at the baker's house. Crafts were made in workshops, but with people in a circle not along a production line. Markets were places where people dealt face to face. Business was a living system.

When work is cut off from life, when shops or cafes become like machines, they are diminished. Efficient, yes. Good for people, no. Visit a leading edge office like WeWork or an artisanal cafe and you see the older idea of work and life returning. As sociable as a bee hive. And as productive too.

How to capture such a trend for the BETTER? By making a business book that is closer to life, less boring, formal. Forget management science. What about the art? Let's take the suit and tie off. Be human. Breathe.

2

how business is getting better 151

1
why business is getting better

1.1

the ethos of care

Business and society in the modern era has been dominated by the ethos of competition; from business strategy and social darwinism to competitive aspirations for 'cool' or 'status'. This helped us get where we are today. But the challenges of tomorrow require a different ethos. They demand that we care. For the ecosystem. For the poor, old and marginalised. For each other, our neighbours and families.

an ethos of care

According to proponents of this idea, after 200 years of mechanical materialism (and all the benefits and problems it has brought) humanity is rediscovering its actual humanity in the form of an ethos of care.

CARE is a feeling for; empathy, regard, respect and compassion for other people but also a feeling for making, for serving, for nature, for playing...

CARE is a feeling; the essential social emotion that bonds us all in a subtle web of interdependence with reciprocity, affection and mutual regard.

Proponents argue that **CARE** is the most characteristically human trait – that it is more than a belief: it is an innate disposition to act in certain ways.

They also argue for the return of care as answering a need for a wiser more mature humanity, feeling as a single human family, feeling for earth and other species.

"If the human being is not cared for from cradle to grave, the human being becomes unstructured, wastes away, loses its bearings in life and dies. If, during life, the human being does not do with care everything it engages with, it will end up jeopardising itself and destroying that which is around it. It is to care. Part of the human essence, and this fact answers the very question: What is it to be a human being?"

Essential Care: An Ethics of Human Nature by Leonardo Boff (2008)

"There are a number of qualities which are important for mental peace, but from the little experience I have, I believe that one of the most important factors is human compassion and affection: a sense of caring."

Dalai Lama: quoted in Hearing the Call Across Traditions, edited by Adam Davis (2009)

"In the different voice of women lies the truth of an ethic of care, the tie between relationship and responsibility, and the origins of aggression in the failure of connection."

Carol Gilligan: In a Different Voice (1982)

"The Empathic Civilization is emerging. A younger generation is fast extending its empathic embrace beyond religious affiliations and national identification to include the whole of humanity and the vast project of life that envelops the Earth."

Jeremy Rifkin, The Empathic Civilization (2010)

a feeling for...

(emerging trends that are part of a softer more care based culture)

causes

Single issues mobilise millions of advocates.

collaboration

From *Kickstarter* to peer to peer lending.

intimacy

A culture of connecting through revealing not concealing.

local

Farmers markets and 'Made in Brooklyn'.

hospitality

Home as popup restaurant, new services that delight.

natural

Nothing artificial, biophilic design.

sharing

Sharing of stuff e.g. AirBnB. Sharing in social media.

experiences

From possessions to peak experiences.

artisan

Appreciating and making from latte art to chocolate.

care is the new cool
a feeling with...

'Cool' was the idea of standing out:
being different and better than others.

Cool was cold and distant.
Based on the gaze not the touch.

Art critic John Berger described this
visual modernist consumer culture as being
grounded in envy.

'Cool' promised to make each of us feel
like a rock star just through acquiring the
right jeans or haircut.

Whereas the hipster brands of today
are more about being yourself.

sphere of intimacy
& disclosure
of private lives.

Trends to feeling with
and a more convivial,
collective culture include...

community
& ad hoc crowds
around enthusiasms.

authenticity
& the rejection
of artificial.

social
validation
& every decision weighed
for likes.

sustainability
& causes that matter
to people.

approachability
& casual decor,
dining, workplaces.

play
& injecting fun,
spontaneity, freedom.

if you want to know what people will value tomorrow then you only have to **look at what young people value today**

%

of all under 30s live in

emerging developing markets

PWC Global CEO Survey

73%

of global millennials are willing to pay more to buy from those making a positive social or environmental impact (a big increase from 50%, 2014).

Rates were lower in North America and Europe than in the Middle East, Africa, Asia, and Latin America.

"Consumers in developing markets are often closer to and more aware of the needs in their surrounding communities as they are reminded daily of the challenges around them, which leads to a desire to give back and help others."

3x more favourable to sustainable brands than 35–49 year olds

12x more favourable to sustainable brands than 50–65 year olds

89%

of young people globally believe
men and women should be

treated equally

... and not just in the west

china (94%) india (92%) brazil (91%)

all scored higher than usa and uk

According to the Financial Times (8/2/17) Emerging Market Youth Embrace Liberal Globalism. West lags behind in levels of happiness, optimism and tolerance.

"We can no longer generalise about conservative developing countries and more liberal developed countries."

Emerging market youth are also more socially conscious.

Top ten countries where youth agreed making
a wider contribution to society is very important:

1	brazil	86%
2	india	83%
3	israel	79%
3	turkey	79%
5	indonesia	78%
6	china	75%
7	argentina	73%
8	usa	71%
8	nigeria	71%
10	italy	69%

Data from a 20 country survey by the Varkey Foundation
of young adults born between 1995 and 2001.

the balancing pole and the safety net

clinical health
and psychology
focus on fixing illness

like a safety net
catching us if we fall ill

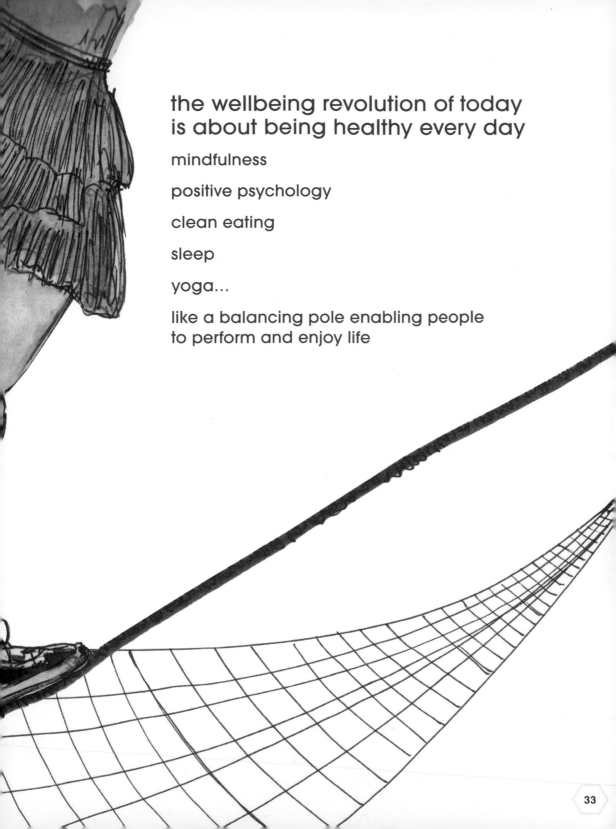

the wellbeing revolution of today
is about being healthy every day

mindfulness

positive psychology

clean eating

sleep

yoga...

like a balancing pole enabling people
to perform and enjoy life

a new wave of wellbeing

We are in the midst of what some have called 'a wellbeing revolution': natural and functional foods, alternative therapies, meditation and much more besides. This is more than a series of fads as there is an underlying shift in our understanding of health, what we eat, happiness, sleep... from a reductive Western medical-scientific view based on treating isolated conditions to a holistic sense of wellness being about a whole mind-body-person and their lifestyle.

a wellbeeing
revolution

3 dimensions of wellbeeing

social
Social & sharing
Social purpose
Liberal social values
Social wellbeing

natural
Not processed
Revival of traditions
Experience of nature
Local and authentic

wellness
Clean eating
Mindfulness
Balance & vitality
Sleep and de-stress

John Grant

We are a social species. We need much more than good food and fitness to thrive. Especially when many of us work with ideas and relationships, not physical labour. We need achievement, belonging, a stimulating environment, contact with nature, happy communities, a sense of purpose.

Let's call it 'Wellbeeing'. And if people are like bees then companies are like hives; factories of social wellbeing (or its lack).

In 2015 avocados overtook oranges in the UK retail fruit sales chart.

president obama
@potus

following

respect the nyt, but not buying peas in guac. onions, garlic, hot peppers, classic

Reply   Retweet   Favorite   More

15,370
retweets

21,423
favourites

"some have called it a wellness revolution. in 2015, we had wearable fitness, farm-to-table, bean-to-bar, green juicing, kale and avocado with everything and mindfulness everywhere."

Daily Telegraph

"I believe the gut is the gateway to health, and the first step I take with all of my patients regardless of their diagnosis is to heal the gut. 60-80% of our immune system is located in our gut, gut imbalances have been linked to hormonal imbalances, autoimmune diseases, diabetes, chronic fatigue, fibromyalgia, anxiety, depression, eczema, rosacea, and other chronic health problems."

Dr Amy Myers

"Food is medicine.Bad food is bad medicine and will make us sick. Good food is good medicine that can prevent, reverse, and even cure disease."

Mark Hyman, MD

"stomach is the home of disease and diet is the main medicine."

it's all about the gut

digestive health

good bacteria

inflammation

liver function

leaky gut

This is why alternative health practitioners advise removing foods that can be inflammatory (including gluten, sugar, corn, soy, dairy) and why there is such a fuss about fermented foods (like kombucha, and juice detoxes).

usa

of adults are trying
to cut gluten

DR WILLIAM DAVIS

NO.1 BESTSELLER

WHEAT BELLY

THE EFFORTLESS
HEALTH AND
WEIGHT-LOSS
SOLUTION

✓ NO EXERCISE
✓ NO CALORIE COUNTING
✓ NO DENIAL

WHEAT BELLY · DR WILLIAM DAVIS

less than **½**

of young adults drank
alcohol in the last week

Alcohol free events such as comedy tour The Shine, and morning
raves are increasingly popular in hip cities like London and New York
with a new generation who want to have all the fun and sense
of freedom of a good party, without getting trashed.

The Independent 15.01.16

The Paleo diet is one of today's most telling diet trends. The idea (from radiologist Stanley Boyd Eaton and anthropologist Melvin Konner) is to eat what our ancestors evolved to eat rather than modern farmed crops; less farmed (grain and dairy) and more hunted (meat) and gathered (fruit and vegetables). Other popular diets (like 'low carb' and 'eating clean') feature similar food types. A broader shift being from 'processed' foods towards authentic, natural, local. Of which 'Paleo' arguably is the logical conclusion?

good. clean. **goop.**

Film star Gwyneth Paltrow influences millions through her blog "Gloop" which combines lifestyle and fashion trends with healthful tips and recipes.

Bruno Rondinelli

Researchers looked at data from over 136,000 study participants, mainly from the United States and Japan. The US studies evaluated a sense of purpose and meaning in life while the Japanese studies looked at the concept of "IKIGAI," translated as "a life worth living."

Even after adjusting for other factors, the researchers found that the mortality rate was about one fifth lower for participants who had reported a strong sense of purpose.

thescienceexplorer.com

John Grant

1 in 5

Americans aged 4 years and over had at least one complementary health approach, which could include massage therapy, tai chi, chiropractic manipulation, homeopathic treatment, hypnosis and energy healing therapy.

National Center for Complementary and Integrative Health (NCCIH/DELOITTE)

Sleep has become a hot topic, with mattress startups like SIMBA, sleep trackers like Beddit and best selling authors like Arianna Huffington all pushing the idea that getting better sleep is the bedrock of wellbeing.

It's obvious when you look at bees that the health of any individual depends on the health of the hive.

We are now 'discovering' what our ancestors knew: that human health derives from profound interdependence; from relationships, community, contact with nature, purpose.

it's hard to be healthy in a sick society

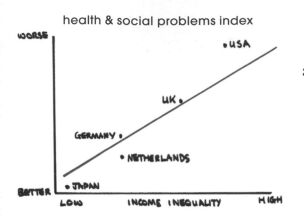

health & social problems index

WORSE

• USA

UK •

GERMANY •

• NETHERLANDS

BETTER • JAPAN

LOW   INCOME INEQUALITY   HIGH

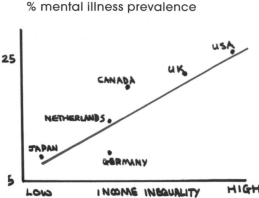

% mental illness prevalence

25

USA

CANADA   UK

NETHERLANDS •

JAPAN

GERMANY

5

LOW   INCOME INEQUALITY   HIGH

The Spirit Level

Why Equality
is Better for Everyone

Richard Wilkinson and Kate Pickett

'A big idea, big enough to change political thinking'
Sunday Times
'A sweeping theory of everything' *Guardian*

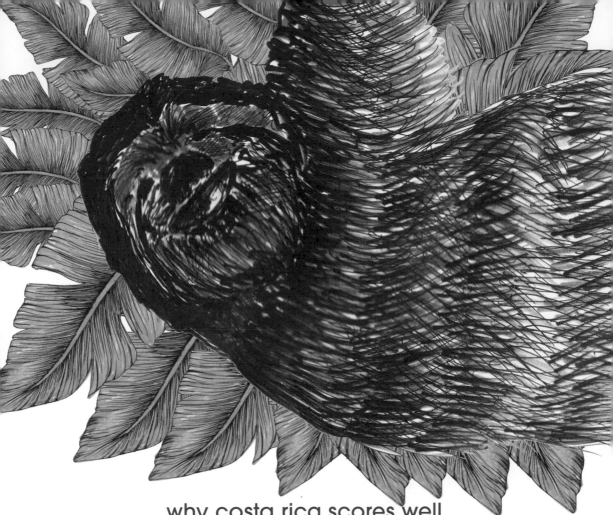

why costa rica scores well on the happiness index

"Costa Rica has no army. It was abolished in 1949. Official figures suggest that it has bucked the trend of losing its forests: more than half its territory is now covered in trees, compared to 20% in the 1980s. But does this "greenness" make Costa Ricans happier? "Yes," says Mr Ulate. "Now I have a simpler, less materialistic life, more in tune with nature." "We don't have a sensation of death," says Mr Montealegre. "Nothing is arid here, you can see life everywhere." He points out that Costa Ricans often answer the question 'How are you?' with the phrase "pura vida". It literally translates as "pure life" but roughly means "cool" or "everything's fine". Analysts say that Costa Ricans' apparent happiness could be down to a whole series of factors in addition to greenness: strong social networks of friends, families and neighbours; ubiquitous social and education programmes; and tolerance of social divisions and different opinions."

BBC News

John Grant

nature grounding

A 2009 study by Kaplan et al showed that walking in the park for one hour increased attention and memory by 20 per cent. Kuo and Sullivan (2001) found that levels of aggression and violence were significantly lower among individuals who had some nearby nature outside their apartments than among their counterparts who lived in barren conditions.

John Grant

people with more social connections live longer

"Social connections not only give us pleasure, they also influence our long-term health in ways every bit as powerful as adequate sleep, a good diet, and not smoking. Dozens of studies have shown that people who have satisfying relationships with family, friends, and their community are happier, have fewer health problems, and live longer. Conversely, a relative lack of social ties is associated with depression and later-life cognitive decline, as well as with increased mortality. One study, which examined data from more than 309,000 people, found that lack of strong relationships increased the risk of premature death from all causes by 50% – an effect on mortality risk roughly comparable to smoking up to 15 cigarettes a day, and greater than obesity and physical inactivity."

health.harvard.edu

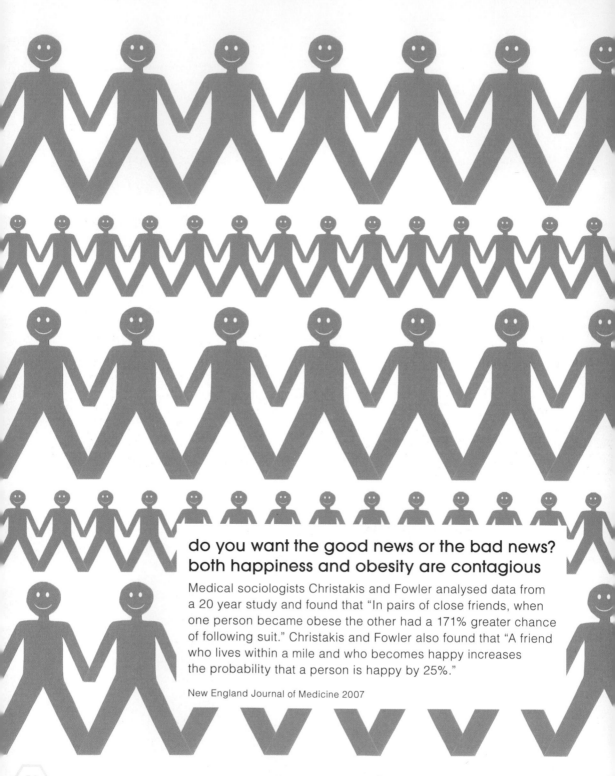

do you want the good news or the bad news? both happiness and obesity are contagious

Medical sociologists Christakis and Fowler analysed data from a 20 year study and found that "In pairs of close friends, when one person became obese the other had a 171% greater chance of following suit." Christakis and Fowler also found that "A friend who lives within a mile and who becomes happy increases the probability that a person is happy by 25%."

New England Journal of Medicine 2007

1.2

causes for concern

Wellbeing has become so precious in our era, precisely because it is in short supply. The old enemies of health like spreading diseases have been eclipsed by stress, obesity, anxiety and chronic illness. Our definition of health itself has shifted (in line with how we work, live and expect to thrive) from mechanical fitness to happiness, emotional resilience, balance and vitality. And while a healthy, active old age is increasingly made possible by medical advances, the youngest generations are the least thriving and most under pressure.

#23

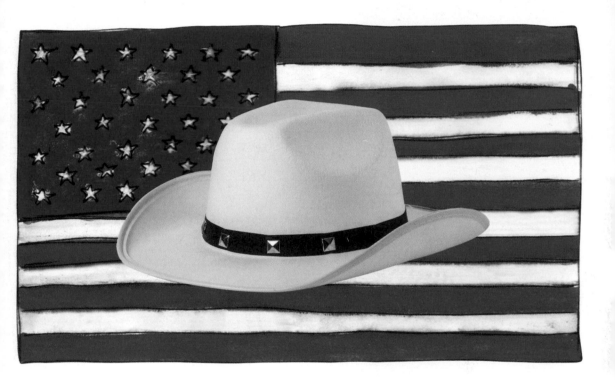

wellbeing world rankings
a tale of two americas

Gallup/Healthways world poll (2014)

80% of wellbeing comes from people, work, society, economy and

%

is physical health (which also relies on society)

The Gallup/Healthways world poll (2014) is the most authoritative global study of the state of wellbeing.

Their Global Wellbeing Index is defined as having five elements based on people's answers to statements describing their life experience and status on various dimensions.

social

Having supportive relationships and love in your life.

purpose

Liking what you do each day and being motivated to achieve your goals.

community

Liking where you live, feeling safe, and having pride in your community.

financial

Managing your economic life to reduce stress and increase security.

physical

Having good health and enough energy to get things done daily.

Countries with strong wellbeing tend to be rounded and perform well on most measures (except financial), but countries with lower scores relative to their economic standing tended to have particular problem areas:

United States fares poorly on physical health, with obesity and chronic illness.

China fares poorly on a sense of purpose and community wellbeing.

UK is 'okay' on most measures but is 44th in world rankings; significantly behind Scandinavia, Holland, Germany & neighbouring Ireland.

gallup/healthway findings 2014

Countries with highest wellbeing scores,
% thriving in 3+ areas of wellbeing

1 panama 53%
2 costa rica 48%
3 puerto rico 46%
4 switzerland 39%
5 belize 39%

interestingly (President Trump take note)
Mexico was #10 whereas USA was only #23

there's a world of difference between
functioning
and flourishing

John Grant

what is wellbeing?

Human flourishing.

Self-evaluation of being comfortable, healthy, happy.

Integrated self development.

Ultimate goal against which 'good' is judged.

Inner resources to cope with stresses

A sense of vitality.

Involved in meaningful activities, contributing to society.

A full life: emotional, physical, social, spiritual.

fewer than

3%

of americans meet
the criteria for a
healthy
lifestyle

Mayo Clinic, March 2016

only **1%**

of people alive today are

thriving

on 3/5 Wellbeing Dimensions, Gallup/Healthways

Cluedo?

1 in 2
americans know how
they will probably die

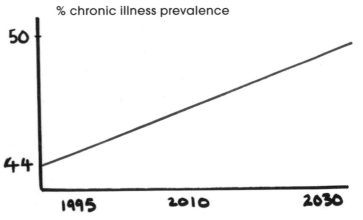

% chronic illness prevalence

50

44

1995   2010   2030

Rand Corporation

we enjoy the idea that
we've made big strides
of progress over the last

200 yrs

and yet we have been less
happy in recent decades
than at any other time since

1800

happiness, uk

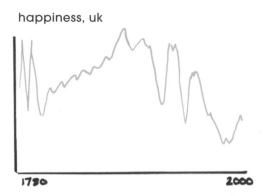

1750   2000

happiness, usa

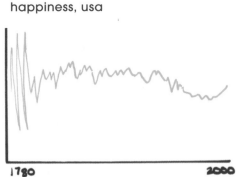

1750   2000

As measured by deriving mood (sentiment)
from written language over time

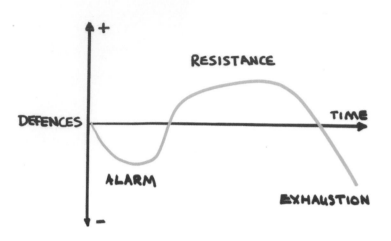

stress is like the woodworm of wellbeing

The term 'stress' was borrowed from physics; meaning 'under strain' by Hans Selye as recently as 1956.

proportion of american adults who report...

physical symptoms caused by stress 77%
psychological symptoms caused by stress 73%
feel they are living with extreme stress 33%
feel stress increased over past 5 years 48%
cited money and work as leading cause 76%
report lying awake at night due to stress 48%

American Institute of Stress

£26BN

annual cost
of stress to uk employers

Sainsbury Centre for Mental Health

Woman at Occupy Wall Street, Timothy Krause

5%

of American millennials are thriving

Gallup

Millennial dissatisfaction with quality of life and lack of opportunity was a major factor in the Arab Spring uprisings. But how are they doing in the richest nation in the world? Not well according to this research....

"Unfortunately, Gallup and Healthways have found that (US) millennials are the generation least likely to be thriving. A mere 5% of working millennials are thriving across all five elements."

the millennial homesick blues

"The job hunt has become millennial version of the Hunger Games".

All Groan Up

"Higher levels of student loan debt, poverty and unemployment, and lower levels of wealth and personal income than any other generation at the same stage of life"

Pew

Younger Americans' delay marriage because of their economic situation. 75% said that financial security should preface marriage.

The Atlantic

3x more young adults are obese compared to the 1970s. 2/3 do not exercise regularly.

Cdc.gov

Millennials are reporting higher levels of clinical anxiety, stress, and depression than any other generation at the same age.

Psychology Today

1.3

business challenges

Business is under a number of pressures which are forcing
the pace and direction of change. Transparency means it can
no longer pretend. While a crisis of trust makes it imperative
to re-engage. Talent is fickle and picky. And every business
is in transformation to adapt to an era of digitalisation,
globalisation and hyper competition. All of these stresses
have led to embracing wellbeing, which gives business
a new way to appeal to people.

cure all

wonder drug

magic bullet

elixir

nostrum

universal remedy

PANACEA

the wellbeing revolution is proving a business

panacea

In Greek mythology, Panacea (Greek Πανάκεια) was a goddess of universal remedy. She was the daughter of Asclepius and Epione. Panacea was said to have a poultice or potion with which she healed the sick. This brought about the concept of the panacea in medicine, a substance meant to cure all diseases. The term is also used figuratively as something intended to completely solve a large, multi-faceted problem.

Wikipedia

wellbeing unlocks four key 21st century business challenges

- transparency
- trust
- talent
- transformation

the emperor's new
transparency

Transparency is about more than information being more readily available. It is about a new sceptical confidence and refusal to be hoodwinked on the part of consumers and their watchdog media and social sources. Mass produced goods can no longer get away with pretending to be something they are not. The truth will out.

A telltale example in the Daily Mirror (2/4/16) was their discovery that the Sainsbury Holme Farm brand venison conjuring "images of animals grazing in meadows and fresh local fare" was actually named after the address of its packaging plant on an industrial estate!

TRUST ME

Nice factories and farms

Lovely place to work

transparency means supporting wellbeing gets recognised

Good products and services

Doing some good in the world

Employees as ambassadors

Sourcing ethics

and that not supporting wellbeing gets recognised too

Disgruntled employees

Customer complaints

Negative reviews

Manufacturing safety

Data privacy policies

Ingredients & health

Profit, pay & tax

Excessive profit margins

55 %

of CEOs are concerned about the

lack of trust in business

vs 37% just three years ago

PWC Global CEO Survey

52%

of the global general public say that they

trust business

Edelman Trust Barometer

"Trust is fragile. Like a piece of china, once cracked
it is never quite the same. And people's trust in business,
and those who lead it, is today cracking."

Charles Handy

Bruno Rondinelli

70 years of building their brand with award winning advertising undone by just one lie

Since the 1950s VW have produced some of the world's most loved brand advertising. Perhaps that is why activist group Brandalism responded to their emissions cheating by posting fake VW posters all over Paris on the eve of Cop21 saying "We're Sorry That We Got Caught". Brand Finance estimated the VW brand lost $10B – one third of its value - after the scandal.

here's why trust is more important than ever.

yesterday was about trusted products.

we had to trust they would work, be safe, not break.

today's trust issues are about

not being ripped off.

we expect amazing value.
we no longer take brands' word
for it. we will google for hidden
catches, negative reviews, pricing.

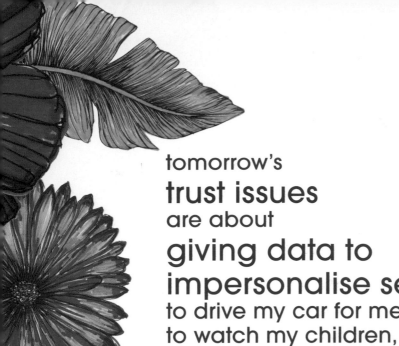

tomorrow's
trust issues
are about
giving data to
impersonalise services,
to drive my car for me,
to watch my children,
manage whole
parts of my life
like health, work or finance.
companies are investing
billions
in these data led business models.
but they only make
sense when people
can get over their
natural weariness.

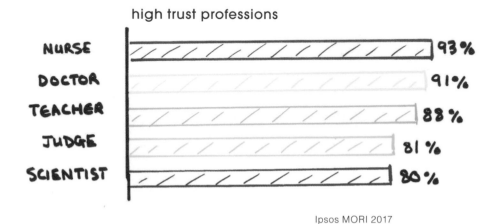

high trust professions

NURSE		93%
DOCTOR		91%
TEACHER		88%
JUDGE		81%
SCIENTIST		80%

Ipsos MORI 2017

we trust public servants
who follow a code

low trust professions

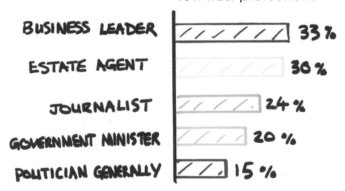

BUSINESS LEADER	33%
ESTATE AGENT	30%
JOURNALIST	24%
GOVERNMENT MINISTER	20%
POLITICIAN GENERALLY	15%

Ipsos MORI 2017

we distrust self
interested fat cats

% believe 'most people can be trusted'

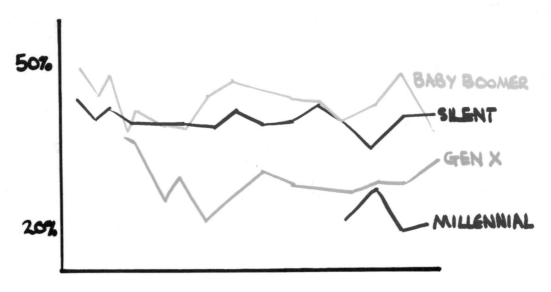

Pew Research Centre

the younger you are the less trusting
this issue is only going to get worse

and #FAKENEWS isn't helping

 the associated press @AP

following

breaking: two explotions in the white house and barack obama is injured

↩ Reply   ⇄ Retweet   ★ Favorite   ••• More

1,181 retweets	52 favourites

A study by the Oxford Internet Institute (March 2017) found that during the US election fake news – which they defined as "propaganda and ideologically extreme, hyper-partisan or conspiratorial political news and information" – was shared as much by Twitter users as professional news.

Fake news can have real effects. This 2013 example (when the AP Twitter account was hacked) caused a 1% dip in the Dow Jones stock index.

50%

of the global workforce
in 2020 will be
millennials

PWC Millennials at Work, Reshaping the Workplace

58%

would choose

work life
balance

over improved financial benefits

$7600

average paycut

millennials would take
for better quality of work life

Fidelity Investments Evaluate a Job Offer Study 2016

talent

three quarters of the 1,300
CEOs interviewed by PWC
rank skills shortage as the

biggest threat

to their business. this is up
from less than half (46%)
six years ago.

this is creating a

'gig economy'

where workers with the most
in-demand skills can dictate
where and when they work,
and who they work for.

PWC global CEO SURVEY 2016

why chase manhattan when you can
change the world?

% harvard biz school graduates go into...

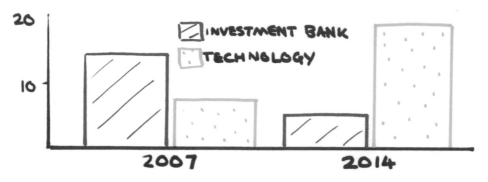

INVESTMENT BANK
TECHNOLOGY

2007   2014

Bloomberg

"I have coffee with a couple hundred students and alumni every year and discuss their careers. Over the past 14 years of my doing this, I've noticed the drastic change in these conversations. Many more of the undergrads and MBAs today are looking into working for NGOs, or at least for corporations which have serious Corporate Social Responsibility programs. This search for meaning and purpose is on the agendas of most Millennials in the Western World and increasingly in the developing economies.

Karl Moore, Forbes Magazine 2014

Job cuts in USA announced by major employers 2016

walmart
17,500 jobs

du pont pioneer
6,000 jobs

intel
12,000 jobs

bank of america
8,000 jobs

cisco
5,500 jobs

macy's
4,350 jobs

transformation

culture eats strategy for breakfast

unfortunately in many organisations
restructuring ate culture for dinner

STOP, Nic Redhead

more haste, more
massive fuck-ups

vehicle recalls / yr ('00)

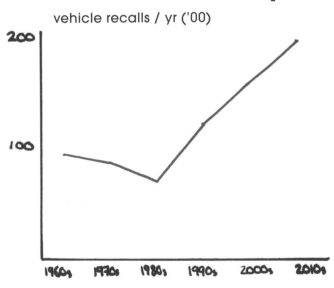

National Highway Traffic Safety Commission

A KPMG survey found that 83% of mergers did not boost
shareholder returns. Studies have shown that there is a relationship
with these financial failures and the all too human costs of mergers.

20-30

major restructurings in europe are
reported in the media every week

according to the European Restructuring Monitor (ERM) database

transformation

a zombie organisation is one where people don't feel safe and regress to primitive survival behaviours

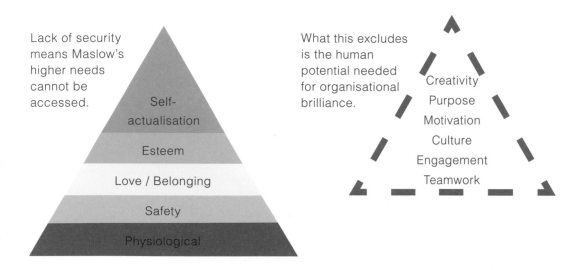

Lack of security means Maslow's higher needs cannot be accessed.

Self-actualisation

Esteem

Love / Belonging

Safety

Physiological

What this excludes is the human potential needed for organisational brilliance.

Creativity
Purpose
Motivation
Culture
Engagement
Teamwork

What is left is defensive, animalistic, feuding, knee-jerk.

slow down

68% of employees were "not engaged" or even "actively disengaged" from their jobs. This had an economic cost to the US economy of $450bn to $550bn.

Gallup

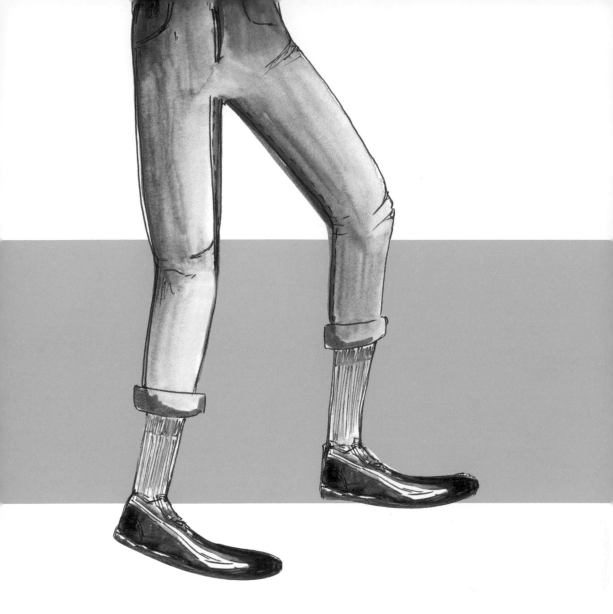

speed up

If you ask the boss of any big American company what is changing his business, odds are he'll say speed. Firms are born and die faster, it is widely claimed. Ideas move around the world more quickly. Supply chains bristle to the instant commands of big-data feeds. Customers' grumbles on Facebook are met with real-time tweaks to products.

The Economist

1.4

better business as cure

Management science used to emphasise that the business of business is business. But now even business schools are calling for social issues to be incorporated into the heart of business thinking. This opens the door to Better business that is commercially thriving and socially positive. How to do this always depends on your starting point. It's about progress not perfection.

just imagine...

business seen as ~~causing~~ curing many problems in modern society

Santander

13000

Shumaiya Khan

80%

agree that "A company can take specific actions that both increase profits and improve the economic and social conditions in the community where it operates." Up from 74% in 2015.

Edelman 2016

"Although trust in business is still low, (global) Millennials see business as the only solution for a better future. They've given up on government. They see big companies as our only hope."

83% expect businesses to do more than they are already doing to help the world, but 82% do believe they are capable of it."

MSL Group 2014

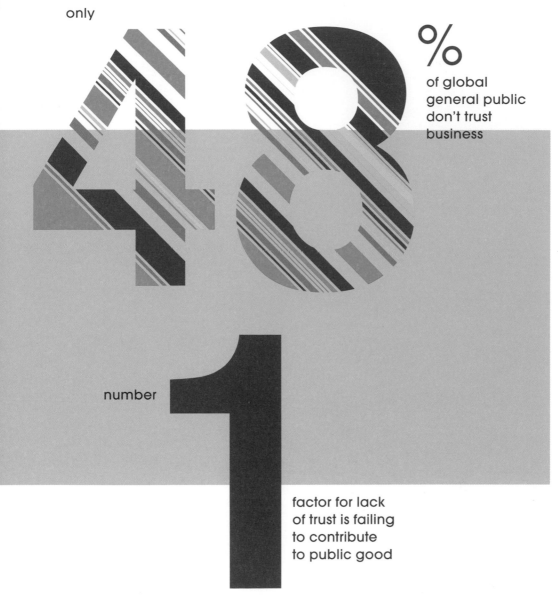

only

48%

of global
general public
don't trust
business

number **1**

factor for lack
of trust is failing
to contribute
to public good

Edelman, 2017

2002

charles handy
harvard business review

Whom and what is a business for?

People get together and exist as an institution that we call a company so that they are able to accomplish something collectively that they could not accomplish separately — they make a contribution to society, a phrase which sounds trite but is fundamental. We hanker to leave a footprint in the sands of time, and if we can do that with the help and companionship of others, so much the better. We need to associate with a cause in order to give purpose to our lives.

2008

ian davis, mckinsey
writing in the economist

Large companies need to build social issues into strategy in a way which reflects their actual business importance. It can help to view the relationship between big business and society in this respect as an implicit "social contract".... This contract has obligations, opportunities and mutual advantage for both sides.

From this perspective, shareholder-value creation or profits are the measure, and the reward, of success in delivering to society the more fundamental business purpose. The measures and rewards reflect the predominant values of the relevant society.

2011

michael porter and mark kramer
harvard business review

business
opportunities

social
needs

shared
value

corporate
assets

Companies... remain trapped in an outdated, narrow approach
to value creation. Focused on optimizing short-term financial
performance, they overlook the greatest unmet needs in the market
as well as...the depletion of natural resources vital to their
businesses, the viability of suppliers, and the economic distress
of the communities in which they produce and sell? It doesn't
have to be this way. Companies could bring business and society
back together if they redefined their purpose as creating "shared
value" in generating economic value in a way that also produces
value for society by addressing its challenges.

2016

 %

 %

of CEOs believe that in five years' time,
successful companies will be guided
by a purpose centred on creating value
for wider stakeholders.

say companies will prioritise long-term
over short-term profitability, and customer
and other stakeholder needs will matter
more than shareholders'.

PWC Global CEO Survey 2016

big business
has a renewed sense of social purpose

vodafone

Contribute to sustainable living by delivering connectivity and innovative services to our customers, 70% of who live in emerging markets.

ford

We go further to make our cars better, our employees happier and our planet a better place to be.

unilever

Make sustainable living commonplace. Grow our business whilst decoupling our environmental footprint from our growth and increasing our positive social impact.

social businesses that start with purpose can often

create progress

even faster

fairphone

We've created the world's first ethical, modular smartphone. You shouldn't have to choose between a great phone and a fair supply chain.

tesla

Produces cars, solar power, home batteries to accelerate the world's transition to sustainable energy.

wholefoods

Embrace our responsibility to co-create a world where each of us, our communities and our planet can flourish. All the while celebrating the sheer love and joy of food.

legal & general have committed to invest £15bn in housing and urban regeneration

"We need a new innovative approach to housing. Helping first time buyers is necessary but not the whole solution. We need to modernise house building and make it more efficient so that we can increase supply and quality for all forms of tenure, and all income and age groups, from students to pensioners. Institutions like Legal & General can regenerate not just residential housing, but the towns and cities in which the homes are built. Infrastructure, jobs and local economic growth are all key to creating thriving communities where people want to live."

Nigel Wilson CEO

NIGHTSHOT 2. University of Salford Press Office

Legal & General have a 50% stake in Salford Media City, one of a growing number of initiatives they have invested in to support the regeneration of cities in the North of England.

mark zuckerberg ✓
27 january at 13:34 · palo alto, ca, united states

my grandparents came from germany, austria and poland. pricilla's parents were refugees from china and vietnam. the united states is a nation of immigrants, and we should be proud of that.

like many of you, i'm concerned about the impact of recent executive orders signed by president turmp

brian chesky ✓
@bchesky

follow

airbnb is providing free housing to refugees and anyone not allowed in the us. stay tuned for more, contact me if urgent need for housing

115,330 retweets	196,206 likes

it wasn't just activists that protested trump's travel ban

american business leaders also spoke publically against it

others included:

apple google microsoft salesforce slack starbucks uber

111

the better manifesto

Better business puts human wellbeing first in every decision.

Better is restless. It aims to improve with concrete steps of progress.

Better is measured relative to the alternatives. You can be a better wholefoods company. But you can also be a better fast food company.

Better is measured by its net result: population wellbeing. If you are a popular sugary food and you move to low sugar, you cut sugar consumption in the population more than a zero sugar product with niche appeal.

Better includes creating prosperity. Refusing to see doing well and creating wellbeing a trade off. Using ingenuity, innovation, sheer determination. The idea being that there is always a better way, if you look hard enough.

Better has an inbuilt unfair advantage: goodwill. Better attracts better people. Who work with a better sense of purpose. And who work better together (because that purpose overrides personal differences and petty conflicts). You relate better to customers, suppliers, communities, even regulators. And you build better brands for an age of transparency with authenticity, trust.

Once you are on the Better path, anything else seems mean and pointless.

negative

part of problem

Undermining physical, emotional and social wellbeing.

reform

neutral

not bad

Acceptable performance on wellbeing.

transform

native

part of solution

Wellbeing leader offering alternatives with no big disadvantages.

perform

how to do better?

it depends on your starting point

Better is progressive; start where you are at (and where your audiences are at) then take steps in the right direction.

40 consecutive quarters of uk growth

warm chicken salad

reform - mcdonalds uk

In the UK, McDonalds has embraced healthier eating with salads and fruit bags, sustainable sourcing, organic, free range, local, recycling... created fresh modern cafe design & earned 'best place to work' awards.

In the USA, McDonalds did none of this and is in steep decline, losing 1/8 of its visits by young millennials in last 3 years.

Technomic Data, 2014

it's better to take people with you than try to be 'perfect'

French supermarket Intermarche launched a sugar detox range using their popular chocolate yoghurt. French people need to reduce sugar consumption by at least half. The aim was to help people experience how easy it is to get used to lower sugar products. As well as selling out immediately and generating 20% increase in store visits, the idea trended in social media and attracted 6 million impressions.

"there can be no reason why man should not make towns liveable and healthy... just as much subject to the beneficient influence of bright sunshine, fresh air, flowers, and plants, as the country."

Lord William Lever, 1898

better purpose

"By 2020 we will help more than a billion people take action to improve their health and well-being."

Unilever Sustainable Living Plan

better principles

"...somewhere around the 1980s I think marketing got lost, and consumerism in its most rampant form became the name of the game of marketers and advertisers. It put stuff first, rather than people."

Keith Weed, Unilever Chief Marketing Officer

better results

Sustainable Living Brands – which have integrated sustainability into both their purpose and products:

- Delivered nearly half Unilever's growth.
- Grew 30% faster than the rest of the business.
- Included Unilever's five biggest brands – Knorr, Dove, Dirt is Good, Lipton and Hellmann's.

Unilever.com

perform: lululemon

Founded in Canada in 1998, Lululemon is a yoga inspired sportswear brand, with revenues of $2.3B, through 400 stores and online. In contrast with sports celebrity advertising strategies of the mega sports apparel brands, Lululemon has been built through community marketing: digital, social media, ambassadors and grassroots initiatives through local stores.

does it make
a difference?

i.e. in people's lives

better is about both

difference
and direction

is it better than
alternatives?

is it recognised
as different?

is it improving
things?

heading in the
right direction

is it inspiring?

making people want
to be better

1.5

a new business culture

The 1990s brought us the Dotcom Boom, vision and value statements, Fast Company magazine, and what one book called 'Funky Business'. Then in the 2000s came sustainability, the War for Talent and 'every company is a software company'. Today those trends have converged into a new business culture that aims to be human friendly inside and out. A culture where it is quite normal to have a Chief Happiness Officer.

"the culture of work is changing. we are living through a period of real transformation. most of our people are millennials and they face different challenges to previous generations. they are hyperconnected, with their entire life on display. older generations don't know what it is like to grow up with that much scrutiny and critique. as an employer, we have a responsibility to help the 600 young adults we will employ today and tomorrow flourish at work. it's our moral obligation really; in return for all their hard work, loyalty and brilliance."

Debbie Martin, Chief Happiness Officer, AND Digital

Employees at AND Digital get to know each other at their new joiners' Bootcamp

leave some
for the rest of us!

Google ranked Fortune's best place to work 7 out of the last 10 years. And (quelle surprise) attracts over 2m CVs/year.

Fortune's Best Place to Work (CAPS)

success may be confirmed
by a few simple measurements
but success itself and the means
to achieve it are a complex system

what is objectionable about mechanical work is the loss of human freedom

A sense of freedom underpins initiative, curiosity, resilience, risk taking, collaboration, loyalty... everything that makes the difference between a business that sleep walks and one that skips along. Any trailblazing entrepreneurial organisation is a collective of people taking responsibility, ownership, pride and credit for its brilliance. There is nothing wrong with pressure, so long as people have the freedom to rise to the challenge themselves. Trying to micro manage your way to increased performance is like trying to accelerate by slamming on the brakes.

Since the industrial revolution, division of labour reduced human work to machine like repetitive actions. It was arguably a poor way to make pins (artless commodities with little value). And it is a terrible way to make design, innovation, software code, service experiences. All of which require human flair, agility, flexibility and initiative. Yet many companies are still organised this way.

there is a more natural way to look at organisations

living

The aim of living creatures and communities being to thrive; not only to preserve wellbeing and internal balance (or homeostasis) but to grow, learn, reproduce, evolve.

social

99% of human genius is social – from our very language, and our ability to learn from each other and store knowledge in shared culture – to our creativity and finer values.

systems

Systems differ from mechanisms in being emergent; having surprising functions of the whole that exceed those of the parts. Like a bee hive functioning to 'farm' whole ecosystems while being made up of creatures barely more sophisticated than flies.

living systems

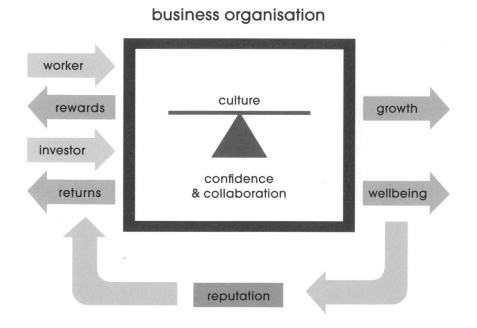

resource

incentive

homeostasis

growth

resource

incentive

nurture
& protect

wellbeing

feedback

business organisation

worker

rewards

culture

growth

investor

returns

confidence
& collaboration

wellbeing

reputation

think of financial results as just an incentive for investors

Jeff Schwartz, former CEO of Timberland would start his investor presentations in Wall Street with the "good news guys – we made our numbers yet again". Before going on to tell them about what really excited him, like their off grid factories, workers' rights, eco transparent labelling…

the old currency of 'success'

money
lean & mean
commodified
unloved

speedy
unconsidered
stressed to gills
accident prone

trendy
undifferentiated
soon to be old hat
superficial

the ethical version
of return on investment

what is your net
contribution to life?

value

wellbeing
resources

is business becoming the bees knees?

Is business becoming the bees knees? There is a general move in this direction. Seeing business in more human terms. But there are some companies making token reforms, while others make sweeping changes. Let's look at a few of the pioneers who have made wellbeing core to what they do and how they do it.

30 years ago this kind of business was a lone pioneer

BEM ESTAR BEM (WELLBEING WELL) = wellbeing + doing good.
A profound philosophy of "inter being" the beauty of being as one.
Partnership a core value partnering with nature, with Amazon Indians
communities (EKOS) with 3 million Natura consultants, with women
entrepreneurship in the favelas. Each product is designed to improve
wellbeing through what founder Luiz Seabre calls 'a semiotic' relating
for instance to acceptance of ageing. A hugely innovative company
with pioneering eco packaging formulations. And it is Brazilian, sexy,
a vision of natural beauty and empathy. The office /factory is in the
forest and is beautifully landscaped with energy shrines, giant
butterflies, toucans in the tree, lots of views into nature.

John Grant

john

"what is the ultimate purpose of your company?"

natura executive

"to create a model of how human societies can function better in 25 to 50 years' time"

137

Sweet Potato
FALAFEL
4.20

CHARGRILLED CHICKEN

AIOLI
4.70

CHORIZO
CLUB
4.95

FLAME-GRILLED BUTTERFLIED
CHICKEN THIGH WITH
OLIVE OIL MAYON
ROCKET & PICKLES
AN ARTISAN SE

COD FILLET FROM SUSTAINABLE SHOALS
WITH OUR OWN TARTARE SAUCE
4.60

PECAN
PIE

TRIPLE CHOCOLATE
COOKIE

naturally fast food

138

sweet Potato
ALAFEL
.95 ✓ WF GF V

MEATBALL
Lunchbox
3.95
✓ WF GF DF

CHICKEN
SUPERFOOD SALAD
5.70 (out) 6.70 (IN) ✓ WF GF

Original
SUPERFOOD
4.75 (out) 5.75
✓ WF GF

CHICKEN

IOLI 🌶
.70 ✓ / WF GF
CHILLI 🌶
.80 ✓ / WF GF
CHORIZO 🐷
LUB
.95 ✓ / WF GF

Thai Green
CHICKEN
CURRY
4.45
✓ / WF GF

CHICKEN & CHORIZO
UB SALAD
.95 (IN) ✓ WF GF

Hummus &
khobez flatbread
2.20 (out) 2.65 (IN)
✓ GF V VN

BETTER
BROWNIE
£1.95
£2.40

NTINE
£1.20
£1.45

CRANBERRY
BAKEWELL
£1.95
£2.40

LEON was named after founder John Vincent's dad and
has always felt like one big happy family, even after 13 years
and growing to 1000 people.

#doing

"It's a non-prescriptive call to action. Every other activewear brand champions this competitive, performance-driven ethos of faster, better, stronger. We believe that Doing Things is better than not doing things. The goal is to integrate activity into your life in a way that's approachable, social and fun."

Tyler Haney, Founder Outdoor Voices

things

LEON

how can fast food be good food?

"We want to make it easy for people to eat well on the high street. We want to do this in every major city in the world."

THE FISH FINGER WRAP

COD FILLET FROM SUSTAINABLE SHOALS
WITH OUR OWN TARTARE SAUCE

4.85 ♥ DF

LEON
fast facts

founded in 2004

2005 winner observer
"best new restaurant"

50 outlets and counting

phenomenal public and
media reaction

"the future of fast food"
Giles Coren, The Times

"i didn't think that fast
food was a good idea,
i was wrong."
Jay Raynor, Observer

LEON

POWER OF PLANTS

no halo

Don't try to be perfect (boring) just be much better than the alternatives at prices that people can comfortably afford.

stealth health

Pioneer better eating with healthy options so tasty and appealing that people choose them without even thinking of the benefits.

under wraps

Work quietly on the things people might not notice but are right things to do; like nitrates out of chorizo.

LEON.
NATURALLY FAST FOOD

SUPER SALAD
LEON ORIGINAL

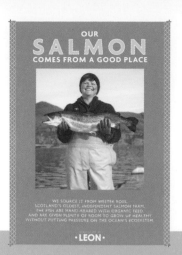

OUR
SALMON
COMES FROM A GOOD PLACE

WE SOURCE IT FROM WESTER ROSS, SCOTLAND'S OLDEST, INDEPENDENT SALMON FARM. THE FISH ARE HAND-REARED WITH ORGANIC FEED, AND ARE GIVEN PLENTY OF ROOM TO GROW UP HEALTHY WITHOUT PUTTING PRESSURE ON THE OCEAN'S ECOSYSTEM.

·LEON·

.LEON.
MANGO
PASSIONFRUIT
KEFIR
SMOOTHIE

LEON

real choices

Don't leave out vegans, freefrom, paleo... these add healthy options anyone can enjoy.

LEON
HAPPY
SALADS
BY JANE BAXTER & JOHN VINCENT

inner child

Bring all the fun and flavour of childhood that people love in fast food – like fish finger wraps – make them healthy delightful, playful.

real innovation

bringing the audience with you is real innovation; fermented drinks, plant based main meals... brought to the mainstream.

no more either or

John helped AND Digital when it was starting out with its brand strategy, name and narrative. The company is now on track to grow to 600 people within its first five years.

AND Digital helps companies accelerate their digital aspirations. They bring the deeply technical skills for building new products and services with their clients. AND also addresses the equally critical human needs of doing this kind of work, helping their clients to build their own capability.

AND Digital quickly made a name for itself, helping clients like ASOS, Vitality, Thomas Cook and Talk Talk get digital faster.

AND Digital has remained a lovely, human, flourishing and welcoming place to work. AND yet managed to create a high performance culture. Balancing hard metrics like profit and growth AND soft metrics like happiness surveys.

winning awards for digital prowess AND human friendliness

so how have they done it?

mindful

Beyond its yoga classes, massages, free fruit and many other initiatives AND Digital pays attention to mental wellbeing, having two or three trained mental health ambassadors per club.

multicellular

AND Digital keeps each individual's workplace experience feeling manageably small and stable, by dividing its operations into clubs and squads. These join, train and stay together. These units can draw on the scale and momentum of bigger and fast growing company.

priority

Policies like wellbeing and community giving have been given priority from day 1, ranked as high as office space, recruitment and marketing. They are treated as essential not nice to have.

empower

The management style
is collaborative. Even the youngest
co worker may have been coding since
they were 8 (and may technically
know more than their manager).
Each is encouraged to lead
their own work.

home

The workplace is modeled
on a family where everyone feels
home. Simple things like ensuring
everyone knows each others' names
and interests. And at 4.44pm every
Friday work stops and the games
commence (hula hooping,
marshmallow tower
building etc.).

recruit well

Recruiters watch
out for skills; but also a bit
of humanity, warmth and kindness.
A fit with the culture. Not based on
being similar to other people but being
open to its values. You can be the
best developer in the world but if
you don't work well with others
you won't work that well at
AND Digital.

2

how business is getting better

2.1

better workplace

Workplaces are shifting rapidly from something akin to battery farming for humans to something much more free range.
This supports better worker emotional and physical health, greater collaboration and even (studies show) better concentration and productivity. And in a competitive fickle market for talent an idyllic workplace and the work lifestyle to go with it is a huge plus.

Google office in Zürich, Marcin Wichary

"How do we have people waking up in the morning feeling really energised and excited about the day ahead? Our workplace vision is to create spaces that just really feel wonderful for people to be in. Places that are vibrant and multi sensory and really touch our soul and make us excited and inspired every day. But also that support not just doing work, but support life."

Anthony Ravitz, Google Real Estate and Workplace Services

Relax! , Alias 0591

chillax

In the knowledge economy, sustainability must extend to the human as well as the environmental level. Many people have seen their ability to balance work with the rest of their lives deteriorate steadily, as they fall victim to the stresses of the long-hours culture. An executive life, some worry, is becoming unsustainable in social terms. We are in danger of populating companies with the modern equivalent of monks, who forgo all else for the sake of their calling. If the contemporary business, with its foundation of human assets, is to survive, it will have to find better ways to protect people from the demands of the jobs it gives them.

Charles Handy, *Harvard Business Review*

what kind of business would
fail to protect their workers?

of usa employers offer

health
schemes

$693

average spend
per employee

Fidelity Investments and the National Business Group on Health

health and safety

exercise classes

stress management

free gym membership

diet advice

workstation ergonomics

healthcare benefits

healthy lifestyle promotion

weight control

best practice in promoting employee health and wellbeing in the city of london

Research Report, City of London Corporation

cycle to work schemes

yoga

sleep education

self esteem

cancer awareness

take the stairs

sports clubs

massages

volunteering

alcohol use

161

"what if people left work feeling better than when they arrived?"

Tidd & Myerson, Wellness 16 Conference

organisations that invested in wellbeing experienced

%

reduction in the cost of employee turnover

%

reduction in the cost of sick leave as well as increased creativity and innovation

Psychological Wellbeing in the Workplace BUPA, 2015.

workplace wellbeing brings amazing results

So it's hardly surprising there are some really innovative entrepreneurs entering this space. For instance,

Stepjockey

stepjockey

A 'gamified' app that encourages people to take the stairs. By counting their steps.

oristand the $25 standing desk

Invented by Hootsuite founder Ryan Holmes who had a bad back and resented paying thousands for standing desks. Simple, portable and funky.

and wellbeing isn't just an
issue for cushy office workers

%

of balfour beatty employees involved in major
projects like motorway construction were

concerned
about work life
balance

of construction workers have

health
concerns

about their workplace according
to a survey by npr magazine

Matthieu Ricard, Founder of Karuna-Shechen, an organization that supports humanitarian projects in the Himalayan region, Festival of Faith

Mindfulness training and meditation have been adopted by employers like Google, Apple, Starbucks, KPMG, Intel, The Home Office. The World Economic Forum was addressed on this subject by actress Goldie Hawn, by French Buddhist monk Matthieu Ricard and neuroscientist Dr Richard Davidson who commented:

"talking about this here at davos would have been unimaginable 5 years ago"

it's not either or

"For far too long we have been operating under a collective delusion that burning out is the necessary price for achieving success. All the latest science is conclusive that, in fact, not only is there no trade-off between living a well-rounded life and high performance, but performance is actually improved when we prioritize our health and well-being."

Arianna Huffington

sick

sick building syndrome is so common it has an acronym

SBS symptoms may include:
Headaches and dizziness
Nausea (feeling sick)
Aches and pains
Fatigue (extreme tiredness)
Poor concentration
Shortness of breath or chest tightness
Eye and throat irritation
Irritated, blocked or runny nose
Skin irritation (skin rashes, dry itchy skin)

www.nhs.uk

Center for Sustainable Landscapes, Phipps Conservatory, 2015-10-10, 02, Dr. Boli

well

A new building standard has been developed to recognise workplaces that make an exceptional positive difference to human health. The first winner of a Platinum WELL certification is the Phipps Center for Sustainable Landscapes; a research and education facility in a landmark public garden whose design is intended to show that natural and human environments need not be incompatible.

bringing plants into
minimalist
'lean' offices increased productivity by

15%

Psychologists found that plants produced better concentration and employee satisfaction and even resulted in improved scores in memory and IQ tests.

"If you put an ant into a 'lean' jam jar, or a gorilla in a zoo into a 'lean' cage, they're miserable beasties. People in lean offices are no different."

"Offices devoid of pictures, souvenirs or other distractions are the most toxic space you can put a human into."

Knight and Haslam, Journal of Experimental Psychology, 2014

free range

environments offer natural light freedom to roam and allow a full range of natural behaviours

be a nicer place
to work and destroy
your competition

one
hire at
a time

Offices at Karma Communications Group, London.

5 Things AND Digital have done to make work more human friendly

1

Divide the company into communities of 84 people (that share an office) and squads of 12 who join and do bootcamp together. The squad is your work family. So that even if the company grows fast "it doesn't feel like that".

SHARE WONDER DELIGHT

2

Building a deliberately diverse workforce in terms of gender, race, nationality – so that there is a richer mix of voices, perspectives and ideas.

Support with individual wellbeing, FitBit challenges, massages and free fruit, talks on sleep, digital detox days... and a big focus on mental wellbeing, including 2-3 mental health ambassadors per club.

Put the human being first. Even people's job titles say their work role AND favourite passion in life. For instance: Paramjit Uppal Founder AND Foodie. Getting the culture right has been a key priority and the organisation was designed and built to be human friendly from scratch.

An industry leading maternity scheme with a particular focus on supporting women when they come back into the workplace; with coaching, support and bonuses to smooth out the expenses of parenthood.

Offices & Employees at AND Digital, London.

super modern but ever so human

At Lloyd's of London the underwriters sit at 'benches' where brokers can come to pitch client business in a back-and-forwards process of deliberation somewhat akin to the legal process but devoted to winning agreement not 'winning a cases'. The format of the market floor enshrines this process in the physical layout.

Selgas Cano Headquarters Madrid, Iwan Baan

want your hq to make a statement?
why not make it an idyll?

Architects Selgas Cano integrated the design of their own offices into lush natural woodland near Madrid, an inspiring setting from which to envisage projects such as their 2015 Pavilion at the Serpentine Gallery.

2.2
better leadership

Since the 1990s a new generation of leaders have brought a new style of leadership – more consultative, empowering, leading from the centre rather than the top. This is a natural approach in Scandinavian, Dutch, Californian and other cultures which have a consensual culture generally. Leaders are learning to lead creatively through storytelling; articulating both uncomfortable truths (Egypt) and visions (Promised Land) and the effortful path needed to get there (crossing the desert).

resilience

metabolism

reproduction

immunity

growth

HORMONES are pervasive, slower, longer acting and they work by activating functions in the body rather than 'knee jerk' commands.

Leadership terms such as empowerment, engagement are more hormonal? It's also down to how in balance you are; taking time for a more measured response?

leaders should be more
hormonal
and less neuronal

fight & flight

movement

micro-management

reactive

NEURONS give quick fire commands, leading to an immediate response. Their effect is short lived, sharp, immediate. Leaders can feel bombarded by organisational demands and there is a temptation to keep firing off hasty responses, being reactive, imposing micromanagement whenever there is a crisis (and around such a leader every drama becomes a crisis)?

overcoming a weakness is the road to true strength

Ben and Jerry's trademark chunky ice cream came about because Ben (Cohen) has a condition called 'anosmia' which means he cannot taste or smell food, so only 'mouth feel' makes eating enjoyable.

the antidote to stuffy tradition

Moderniser CEO Inga Beale brought more than digital transformation programmes and emerging markets expansion, as the first female leader of 329-year-old Lloyd's of London. Beale also instituted a three-day diversity festival, to engage the whole insurance industry in cultural modernisation and attract fresh talent.

Dive In Festival

Dive
In The Festival
for Diversity & Inclusion in Insurance

building blocks of change

In 2004, new CEO Jørgen Vig Knudstorp started LEGO'S remarkable turnaround with a new culture of openness. For instance an early post on his internal blog said:

Shumaiya Khan

"here's my presentation to the board next week any thoughts?"

In his 12 year tenure as CEO the company grew revenues by 17% per year.

plays too safe

naive

every leader has a shadow
which wizard of oz character is yours?

Alamy

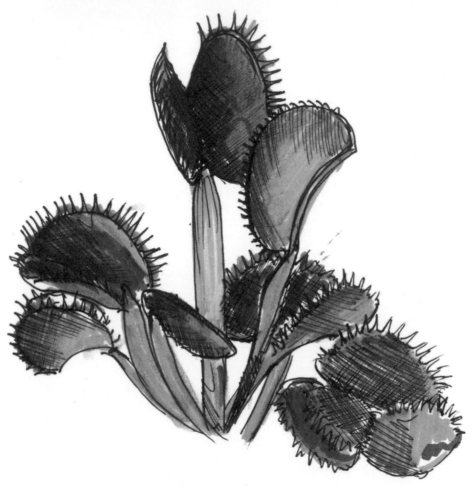

imposter syndrome

In 1978 clinical psychologists Clancy and Imes coined this
term to describe a syndrome among corporate high flyers whose
symptoms included: a fear of being 'found out', trying to conform
or use charm to win approval and a crisis of confidence.
Those affected tend towards perfectionism, micromanagement
and can suffer burnout, anxiety and depression.

it's a leader's job to grasp
uncomfortable new realities

when anders dahlvig took over as IKEA company president....

he was replacing ingvar kamprad (the 'IK' in IKEA). here's how he made the job his own.

1. Codified the IKEA values

2. Distilled the strategy into '10 jobs for 10 years' that everyone understands and can contribute to.

3. Cascaded conversation, what does this mean for us?

4. Framed the change: "I want there to be 100,000 CEOs"

5. Demonstrated principles in action, e.g. a global 'all profits to co-workers day'

6. Decisive symbolic action, women and non-Swedes into highly visible roles.

7. New core challenge, sustainability.

8. Regulated for agility, e.g. "3 person decision rule"

9. Tackle blockages, reduce regional bureaucracy

10. Resilience, commit to not cut at the first sign of a downturn ("learning from last time")

Seeing the organisation not as a hierarchical
static diagram but as a moving story gives
a much better handle on what it is about.
This creates a framework for considering
options and for communicating the direction
in a way each can translate to their own work.

past

what we believe in, what
makes us different and
connects us

present

difficulties that need to
be overcome

leadership

resources

challenges

competitors

reputation

operations

future

vision goals, aspirations
innovations future
generations

the other part that's vital is making
this narrative compelling...

2.3

better strategy

The economy has shifted towards experiences, ideas, services. People can't physically handle much more stuff. And the quality of life quest no longer concerns owning, but being and belonging. This is why wellbeing is now central to strategy. A strategy is a plan to reach a goal. And when that goal is subjective new human experiences then the strategy has to shift accordingly. It's about orchestrating resources around the end customer, rather than an end product.

booming

modern business was built on the dream
of a better material quality of life

US GNP
1945 $200b
1960 $500b

economy

1.5 million
new homes
per year

suburbs

77 million
babies by 1964

birthrate

consuming

post war boom USA bought 1/3
of world's goods and services

Alamy

fashions

frozen food

credit cards

substance

tvs

plastics

cars

kitchens

when western societies were poorer, it was reasonable for economics to focus on how to produce more stuff – that was what societies wanted. yet most people today work in jobs they do not much like, to buy goods they do not much value. what we want is purpose and a sense of continual self-betterment, which is not served by buying another iphone, wardrobe or a kitchen. living in an unfair society is psychologically hurtful; air quality does matter; a workplace where you are respected counts; acting pre-emptively to stay healthy makes sense; life satisfaction is what it is all about.

Will Hutton, Guardian, 31 Jan 2016

THEM AND US

CHANGING BRITAIN —
WHY WE NEED
A FAIR SOCIETY

WILL HUTTON

'Hutton's ability
to articulate
contemporary anxieties
borders on genius'
MARTIN WOLF, *PROSPECT*

BESTSELLING AUTHOR OF *THE STATE WE'RE IN*

according to stev
head of sustainabi
we may have rea

peal

howard
at **IKEA**
hed

stuff

a 2010 study of 3,000 uk parents
by www.dreamtown.co.uk found

238

toys
owned
by typical child

12

number of favourites
played
with regularly

from
having
to being
experiential luxury such as exotic holidays
and gourmet meals now account for

of global luxury spending

Boston Consulting Group

"the secret
to happiness?
spend money on experiences not things"

Forbes Magazine

of millennials would

choose an experience

over buying something

Harris Research

"the instagram generation
perceives every moment as
an anticipated memory."

Daniel Kahneman

63%

of 13 to 23 year olds have
posted their photos of food
or drinks on social media.

YPulse

Crab Fries, Oakland, CA by @shummylafairy on Instagram.

people have a new dream
**buying less
living better**
why not satisfy them?

freddie's flowers
starbucks
pokémon go
samsung gear
hello fresh
airbnb
hyper news

this truly is an experience economy

secret cinema
wework
mixcloud
yplan
snapchat
uber
birchbox

2.4

better technology

Technology has many benefits and also huge positive and negative impacts on wellbeing. Our bodies and minds did not evolve to be always on and 85% of people report suffering from technostress. In technology companies (especially consumer technology like wearables and the smart homie) the race is on to create more intimate, enriching, empowering and less intrusive tech experiences; or as Wired magazine put it: to 'make tech human'.

information technology

side effects may include: anxiety, weight gain, sleeplessness, addiction, headaches, tension and inability to concentrate.

always on edge
where are usa adults using smartphones

Harris/Jumio

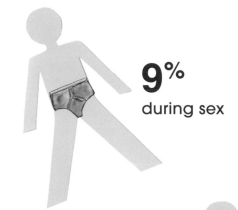

9%
during sex

33%
on a dinner date

12%
in the shower

35%
in a movie
theatre

55%
while driving

even for machines, 'always on' is a bad idea

Psychologists at the University of Hamburg measured their subjects' level of stress hormone cortisol. When expected to be available via email, cortisol levels were significantly higher.

19%
in a church/
place of worship

32%
at a child's/
school function

email like caffeine is best avoided in the evening

"Our brains were never designed to be always on and permanently connected with the amount of stimuli that we get from social media, gaming, constant news updates. And that's a problem."

Dr Max Blumberg, Goldsmiths

39%

of usa employers offer
sleep classes

the french government is regulating

against out
of hours email

sugar stimulates instinctive neural pleasure and reward systems, creates a buzz followed by feeling slumped, is addictive and harmful used in excess.

remind you of anything?

85%

suffer from technostress

Rosen and Weil (1997) define TechnoStress as "any negative impact on attitudes, thoughts, behaviours, or body physiology that is caused either directly or indirectly by technology".

Technostress levels (the proportion of subjects in the general public affected) have shown marked increases since the early 1990s when first measured. Rosen and Weil found 35% in 1992 and 43% in 1995. Recent studies have found much higher levels with the average of 6 studies in 2013 being 85%.

This is likely to reflect the proportion of the population using new technologies (such as mobile, or a work PC), the intensity and length of involvement, the types of interaction and their cognitive demand but also frustrations inherent in keeping up.

you used to have to keep up with the joneses

now you have to keep up with the zuckerbergs

consequences of technostress

1. physical

Adrenaline and noradrenaline
level increases, along with heart rate,
blood pressure.

2. cognitive

ADT (attention deficit trait); individuals
being so overwhelmed by information
that their attention and decisiveness
is significantly reduced.

3. emotional

Research found 50% of time spent
on a computer involves the user
recovering from frustration.

4. loss of control

Research found one in three computer
users felt overwhelmed by technology.
When feeling overwhelmed rather than
viewing an additional task as challenging,
they view the task as a threat.

interestingly... it's worse for the young

Contrary to the image of 'digital natives' a recent study
(Mawhinney, 2015) found

10 to 25 year olds

technostressed

over 25 year olds

technostressed

This suggests that ambient exposure
to technology and rate of adoption of new
technologies might in itself be stressful
(as opposed to degree of 'fluency')?

two directions for
better technology

1.humanify
Less alien, jarring, more flowing, intuitive, ambient, matched to innate human needs & ways.

get out of the way of my life

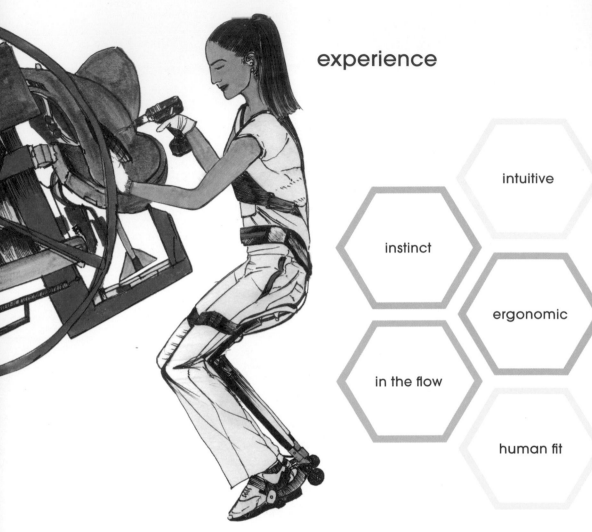

experience

intuitive

instinct

ergonomic

in the flow

human fit

At Audi's assembly plant in Neckarsulm, Germany, workers are testing a new technology called the "chairless chair." Created by Swiss startup Noonee, this carbon-fibre construction allows employees to sit without a chair or stool. At the same time, it improves their posture and reduces strain on their legs.

instead of teaching people technology why not teach technology some humanity?

User experience design is born out of the realisation that how people interact with and experience technology has to start with human habits, biases, limits, instincts and desires if it is ever to become a natural part of daily life.

value engineered

selective

specialised

dedicated

just so

curated

from smart phone to part phone

Kindle and Go Pro by offering just one part of what a smart phone does are able to offer something better for specific uses.

two directions for
better technology

2. magic
Enrich real life, be more than
a distraction, solve problems,
engage emotions.

help me live
a better life

the internet of things (billions of smart physical objects joining the information network) may sound technical to the point of dull but it is capable of bringing quite magical human experiences, like:

dorothy

From ISL Labs. Click your heels (with a smart controller in your shoe, that is linked to your smartphone) and summon an Uber.

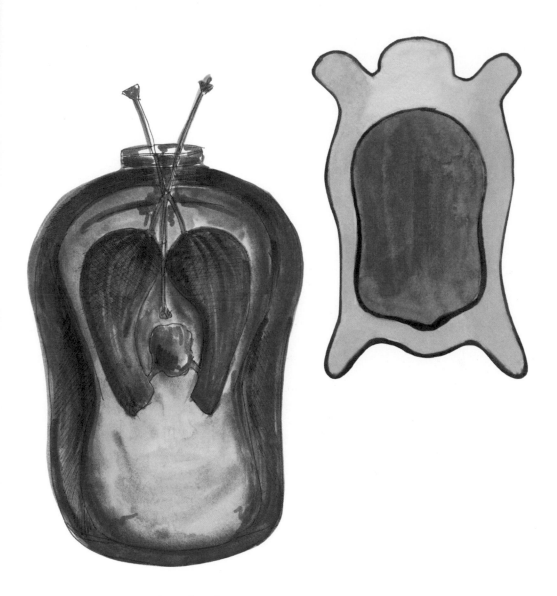

babybe

A gel mattress transmits the heartbeat and breathing from the mother to a premature baby in a hospital incubator.

2.5

better brands

Brands used to be about projecting an image. A factory made cake could be presented with imagery connoting traditional baking, loving mothers, naughty indulgence. Now increasingly people see the cake for what it is. And a new generation of brands are growing up that are authentic in sharing little truths about the way the cake is made, its sourcing, provenance or health (for instance gluten free bakeries are booming). In this see-through world it is vital to differentiate what you offer, the experience, your company. The alternative is to be dragged into a downward spiral of pressured margins and questionable decisions. Branding is dead, but long live the brand.

be one
of a kind

if you want to be kind

There is no 'floor' if you accept commodification and compete in the global race to the bottom. You need to sell something unique, in the age of Google shopping and Chinese copycats. Even low price leaders like IKEA, Target, Lidl sell unique products you cannot buy elsewhere. As do Warby Parker, Netflix. made.com.

It's a moral choice. Only if you are unique will you have the margin to be better.

why be
mean

John Grant

when you can be
meaningful

mean

not valued
sell sell sell
fabricated
optimised
commodity
low margins
exploit

meaningful
valued
followed
authentic
maximised
unique
decent margins
empower

meaningful makes a virtuous circle

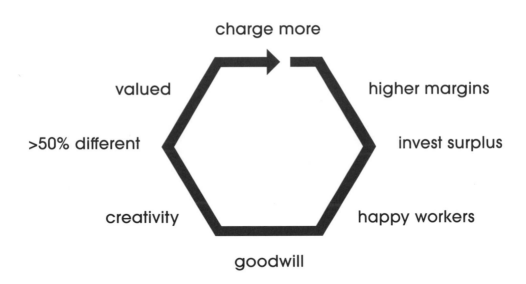

charge more

valued

higher margins

>50% different

invest surplus

creativity

happy workers

goodwill

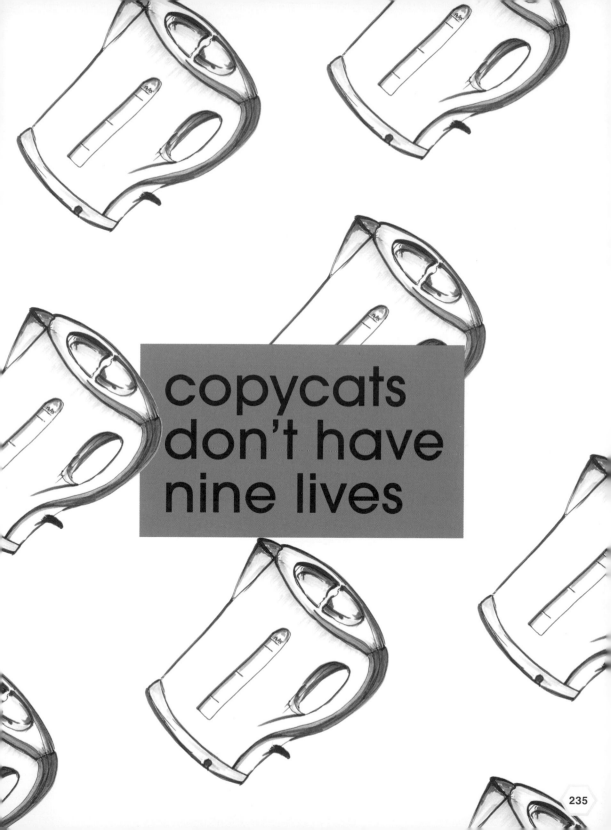

copycats
don't have
nine lives

finding a beautiful coincidence

john:

"what is the business model of the body shop?"

anita roddick:

"we put all the money into the product not the packaging"

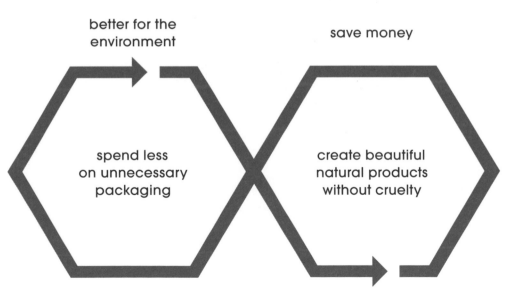

better for the environment

save money

spend less on unnecessary packaging

create beautiful natural products without cruelty

better value for cash-strapped core audience of teens and young mums

help people
achieve wellbeing

Alamy

Tata Trucks in India created a condom brand and education
campaign to help stop the spread of AIDS among truck drivers
and sex workers. The brand name DIPPER comes from
the sign already painted on many Indian trucks' rear bumper
"Use Dipper at Night" (meaning dip your headlights).

2.6

better innovation

Innovation used to be thought of as new product development. But these days it is usually more about developing whole new systems – for instance services (Uber), know how (Genius Bar), or different business models (Prime). Why? Because that's what you have to do these days to create something with tangible difference that is valued. Working with whole systems gives you much more chance of boosting wellbeing too. Because piecemeal products that don't address broader lifestyles and habits of thought seldom work.

plant lots
of small
initiatives

adapt to
changing
conditions

study the
context, what will
it support?

harvest
resources
to reinvest

innovation today
is about whole systems

it's a lot like gardening

recognise
threats and act
promptly

design
parts to solve
each other's
problems

select and
scale what's
thriving

it's not junk

John worked with the Royal Mail to develop a scheme whereby unaddressed mail could be taken to local schools and recycled to be turned into exercise books. Research showed this simple added step transformed attitudes to junk mail and also enabled schools to teach children and families about recycling.

simplistic fixes can come back and bite you

the cobra effect

Under British rule concern rose about the number of cobra snakes in Delhi. Surely something could be done? A bounty was offered for every dead cobra. But then poor people started breeding cobras for reward. The government found out and stopped the bounty. Cobra breeders set free their now worthless snakes. The wild cobra population boomed as a result.

seeing things first person is the first step in innovation

For a workshop with the leadership team of Kingfisher, the home improvement retail group, John got each individual to bring photographs of 'your most shameful storage area at home'. When the laughter died down they had some seriously good ideas based on the insight that "the problems are way too extreme to sell people a few shelves. We need to provide a storage service."

even a soap factory
can change the world

People Against Dirty (PAD), formed by the merger of Ecover
and Method, is one of the most enlightened, fun and innovative
companies John has ever worked with. Here are a few glimpses
of their company culture. Starting with their (eco building award-
winning) new factory, creating jobs in the run down district
of Chicago that once used to make the Pullman trains.

Method - Gotham Greens

innovation comes easier
if you have the right attitude

"We are people against dirty® (PAD), and we've always done things differently. We are fearless thinkers, mad scientists and adventurous designers who believe that making soap leads to brave ideas, bold inventions and beautiful bubbles. We are small, but we have big plans to make the world a cleaner, greener, more colorful place. Our company name is our mission and it's bold and challenging. We are a values led business in every sense, caring as much about the 'how' every bit as much as the 'what'."

raw agility

The company prides itself on its David vs Goliath profile compared to the soap giants. When P&G might take several years to research, develop, brand and consumer test a new product, Method aims to get it out there in a few weeks.

people power

The Method founders Eric and Ryan were friends since childhood and a big part of their success has been making a happy workplace where people can shine.

dream big

The founders aimed high from the start. Their packaging was created by famous New York design Karim Rashid. And instead of targeting niche health food store distribution the pair went out and won space in Target.

breath of fresh air

Free from nasty chemicals for
your children and pets to breathe.
And bringing the creativity and flair
of a hip lifestyle brand
to a boring category.

the future factory

The LEED Platinum award
winning new factory in Pullman,
Chicago is the jewel in their crown.
Bringing much needed jobs
to a downtrodden district
in the former industrial
heartland of America.

2.7

better society

Companies are increasingly aware that their impacts on society at large and their relationships with the communities around them are critical. Big companies have previously managed this by creating a specialist 'CSR' department. Often as a subset of corporate communications. But these days the consensus is you need to be 'doing well by doing good' at the heart of your main business activities.

5 ways to support
human progress

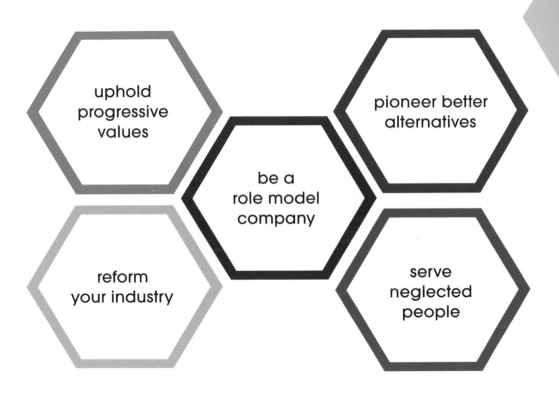

uphold progressive values

pioneer better alternatives

be a role model company

reform your industry

serve neglected people

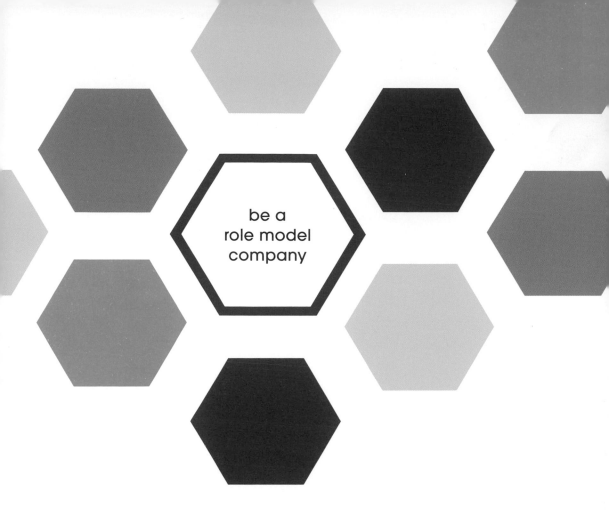

be a
role model
company

Unless you are the next Google your greatest influence
can be if you become an inspiration for other businesses.

And hey, the publicity involved won't hurt you either!

Being the ethical leader in your category can make you
stand out and be trusted. It can help with attracting talent.
Can justify a premium. Or attract new partners.

But how to do this in a way that isn't 'greenwash'?

One answer is to hold yourself accountable by using
an external objective standard. 1600 companies have signed
up to BCorp which aims to be for business what FairTrade
is for coffee; based on social and environmental performance,
transparency, accountability.

serve
neglected
people

Businesses tend to follow the money. That's why positioning decisions (what you do for who) can become an ethical pivot for your whole organisation.

Positioning can lead to global injustices like more R&D money being spent on cosmetic treatments than on malaria. And it can also lead to hugely crowded over-competitive luxury niches. While social needs with global scale are neglected.

To paraphrase Plato, nether regions are the cradle of innovation. The future of mobile money is being developed in Kenya (MPESA) and financial services for the migrant working unbanked (Monese). The last place to 'get' mobile money is a bank.

pioneer better
alternatives

People can only choose among what's on offer.

It's alternatives that create tipping points in markets whether
it is free from foods or Fairtrade. And just as with consumers
there are early adopters among the providers – those willing to move
on something before the research says that "everyone wants this".

Like LEON being the first to bring veganism, fermented foods
and paleo bars into a high street fast food outlet.

uphold
progressive
values

Brands can play a powerful role in 'speaking truth to power'.

AirBNB for instance was one of many leading American companies that spoke out against Donald Trump's travel ban. Not only (as with Facebook and others) did their founder make personal comments in social media. But they invested in a high profile ad campaign, using a TV spot in the Superbowl to underline their commitment to diversity with the slogan #weaccept.

**reform
your industry**

Companies can also quietly redefine what people expect of them.

Ernst & Young. Of the big four accountancy firms it is the one which most espouses restraint and respectability – 'Quality in all we do'. It's not known for a progressive social edge. But it should be.

EY is one of the leading organisations in the world for diversity policies, winning numerous awards for their LBGT policies and similar. They pioneered new protocols for recruitment in the social media era, to ensure that people get chosen on merit not identity or personal lifestyle choices.

conclusion: the bees knees

How do you incorporate all of this into your organisation tomorrow?

Don't worry – you won't need a heart transplant. Culture is not something you can 'change' in a simple way, like throwing a switch. Culture is the life of an organization and exists beyond its hierarchies of control. Culture hence is not 'changed' so much as it is revitalised, regrown, nurtured, sparked into life...

And it turns out that most organisations are already full of people that care. Or who want to. It's innately human to want to be nice. Consistent with self esteem to want to do a good job. To empathise with and respect other human beings. Only corporate constraints were holding that innate tendency to care back.

In all the companies I've ever met who best express the value of care, what they have done is give licence or permission to the natural tendencies of people to care; about their work, their customers and colleagues.

All you have to do then as a leader is create the space to let this happen. Perhaps you could start by demonstrating the value of care in your own behaviour.

Put the book down now. And go and pay somebody you work with a long overdue compliment.

index

supporters

Unbound is a new kind of publishing house. Our books are funded directly by readers. This was a very popular idea during the late eighteenth and early nineteenth centuries. Now we have revived it for the internet age. It allows authors to write the books they really want to write and readers to support the books they would most like to see published.

The names listed below are of readers who have pledged their support and made this book happen. If you'd like to join them, visit **www.unbound.com**.

Amara Aadam
Samee Aadam
Sheena Abbot-Davies
Adam Abrahami
Aladin Aladin
Jon Alexander
Charlotte Anderson
Sarah Anderson
Maite Arango
Hayley Ard
Cindy Barnes
Gemma Batterby
Beth Bell
Oliver Bernath
Lill Bölte
Iain Bonehill
Daniel Bougourd
Clare Brass
Dorothy Brooks
Stephen Brown
Claus Buhl
Dan Burgess
Marcus Butcher
Steve Cassar
David Caygill
Elaine Chambers
Chris Childs
Tracey Rawling Church
Florea Claudiu
Katherine Clements
Mooncup Ltd
Claire Coady

Paul Colman
David Colom
ANDigital Company
Jon Cope
Pilar Cortizo
Chris Coulter
Mark Cowan
Britta Cox
Kate Cox
Dan Cresta
Gavin Crouch
Shenaz Currimjee
Matthew Curtis
Anders Dahlvig
Steve Dawson
Dino Demopoulos
Josh Dugdale
Mark Earls
Leslie Edelman
Michael Ellis
Ben Essen
Stefan Fairbrother
Mahreen Ferdous
Adam Ferrier
James Flint
Christie Franchi
Celia Francis
Chris Friend
Dan Germain
Lucy Gilbert
Ed Gillespie and the lovely folks at Futerra
Damian Glover

Jason Gormley
John Grant
Joy Green
Jessica Greenwood
John Griffiths
Erica Grigg
Christophe Guibeleguiet
Mark Hadfield
Laura Hagan
Dave Hampton
Mark Hancock
Jordan Harper
Gill Harris
Mary Hart
David Hawksworth
Benny Hermansson
Susan Hill
Adrian Ho
Andy Hobsbawm
Mark Hogarth
Janice Holve
Adrian Hosford
Alexandra Howe
Katee Hui
J. Walter Thompson
Verity Johnston
Jon Jones
Gareth Kay
Dave Kelly
Katarina Kempe
Romy Kenyon
Jane Kersel

Matthew Kershaw
Dan Kieran
Simon King
Caroline Knights
Nazanine Ladjevardi
Oliver Lawder
Ramona Liberoff
Ragnar Lidin
Joel Lim
Adam Lotz
Scott Lukas
Paul MacFarlane
Dr Denry Machin
Louisa Mann
Nikki Marshall
Imogen Martineau
Paul Massey
Christian Mathieu
Jacqueline McCouat
Rosalyn McGregor
Karim Melaouah
Lexi Metros
Patrick Mills
John Mitchinson
Miguel do Valle
David Morley
Patrick Morrison
Karen-Babette Müller
Steffen Vander Mynsbrugge
Matti Naar
Carlo Navato
Matthew Neilson

Eirini Nousia
Ramon Ollé
Leonora Oppenheim
Adah Parris
Geoff Patterson
Linda Peters
David Pharo
Joe Pine
Justin Pollard
Carly Reisner
Cyndi Rhoades
Ellen Richardson
Sherry Roberts
Charlie Robertson
John Robson
David Rodriguez
Marc Rogoff
Roberta Ronsivalle
Greta Rossi
Laura Rudoe
Suveen Sahib
Claire Schrader
Katie Scotland
Sven Segal
Colin Sempill
Narda Shirley
Haluk Sicimoglu
Lea Simpson
Mikko Siukosaari
Joanna Skantze
Paul Skinner
Andrew Smart
Jeremy Smith

Barret Stanboulian
Lisa Steel
Superson
Graeme Sutherland
Phil Teer
Al Tepper
Andrew Thornton
Dan Thwaites
Solitaire Townsend
Ville Vainamo
Blaine Vess
Jordi Vilagut
Shazia Walker
Stephen Walker
Henriette Weber
Laura Weston
Hannah Whelan
Donie Wiley
Martin Williams
Louise Wilson
Peter Wilson
Adam Wright